FASTER!
LOUDER!

**HOW A PUNK ROCKER FROM YORKSHIRE BECAME
BRITISH CHAMPION FELL RUNNER**

BOFF WHALLEY

GREAT NORTHERN

Great Northern Books
PO Box 1380, Bradford,
West Yorkshire, BD5 5FB

www.greatnorthernbooks.co.uk

ISBN: 978-1-912101-29-0

Cover design by Boff Whalley

Layout by David Burrill

CIP Data
A catalogue for this book is available from
the British Library

"How are you going to write a book about my life when I can't remember half of it?"

"Well ... the bits you can't remember, the conversations and the details and all that – I'll make those bits up."

"Oh. Alright."

INTRODUCTION

Late November, sometime in the mid 1980s, Gary Devine woke up slowly, desperate for a piss, his mouth stale and dry. It was around seven o'clock, or eight o'clock, or sometime between the two. He wasn't at all sure because he couldn't focus on his watch. His eyes were sore, his head was sore; his whole body was sore, a ringing, humming numbness that comes after a night of extremely loud music and several litres of cider. He was lying awkwardly on a small sofa in someone's living room. A quick, fumbling check: he hadn't puked, and he was fully clothed. Dragging himself up and off the sofa, he got to his feet and looked around the sparsely-furnished room. No people, just a battered three-piece suite, a record deck and a wasteland of empty glasses, squashed cans, erupting ashtrays, teacups, jackets, discarded record sleeves and dirty plates. The last album of the night was still revolving on the turntable, the needle locked in the run-out groove.

Hmmmm click, hmmmm click, hmmmm click, hmmmm click, hmmmm click.

He headed for the doorway and into an uncarpeted hallway, decided against tackling the stairs to the toilet and lurched unsteadily instead towards the front door. Lifting the latch, he flooded the house – whose house, he'd forgotten, or maybe he'd never known – with an intense morning light that drove itself straight between his unfocussed eyes. It had been snowing. Several inches blanketed the street and tree branches bent and stooped under the sparkling crystal weight. No-one was around so he stepped unsteadily across the tiny, tatty front garden and pissed into an unloved hedge. His eyes slowly opened wider against the harsh reflected light and he tried to remember what happened last night.

Cider. Antisect. GBH. Oi Polloi. More cider. Rudimentary Peni's first EP. Conflict, he remembered that. *Mental Mania* on at full volume. Turn it up! Faster! Louder! Conversations and arguments over the music. Spilt drinks in the kitchen. A fight somewhere upstairs. Neighbours from across the street banging on the front door. More cider. A dog slumped in a corner of the hallway, slavering and flinching against the constant comings-and-goings. Some time in the early hours of the morning he'd tried to set the alarm on his watch but his fingers wouldn't work properly, and the buttons were too small. Now it was slowly coming back to him. He was supposed to be awake at 7 to get his kit. To meet Alan. Alan was turning up at his house at 7.30 to give him a lift. Gary looked at the time. Almost 8. Alan would be half a mile away knocking at his front door, ready to give up and get into his Mini and set off in the snow, alone.

He slammed the door shut behind him and huddled into his shirt. The snow crunched under his boots as he stepped out along the front street and up towards his house, breath coming out in clouds. This would wake him up. This would shake him out of feeling dull, and dirty, and sore. He began to jog unsteadily, thinking it might warm him. But Doc Marten's are notoriously slippy in the snow; he slowed back to a fast trudge. Some students – two boys and a girl, all in T-shirts and jeans – were returning from town, laughing, giddy, drunk. One of the boys was singing, loudly, tunelessly, 'Fairytale of New York', even though it wasn't Christmas for another month.

As he reached his house he could see footsteps in the snow leading up the path to his front door. Footsteps leading away again, too. Alan had been and gone.

The front door Yale lock was sticky and temperamental. It had needed fixing for the two years he'd been living there, in the ground floor flat that he shared with a girlfriend and a dog. He stepped into the lifeless house (it smelled of dog food and soup) and, checking the bedroom, saw that both girl and dog were asleep. He grabbed his bag of running gear, his studded shoes and a bottle of water, and quietly left. He was in no fit state to drive, but he had no choice.

An hour later he was standing with almost 200 keen and eager runners on the start line at Rombald's Moor Fell Race, a 6-mile yomp over and around the hilly and freezing Ilkley Moor. The race route would wind its way up to the moortop, slop through snow-covered mud and rocks and descend among the brittle buried heather before returning once more to the skyline. From there it was a long hurtling drop down to a jumble of farm tracks, plunging towards the finish. The hangover, the humming, the numbness, the dry throat, the Antisect and the Oi Polloi and the slavering dog, they all disappeared as the starter, wrapped in an overcoat and scarf, blew a shrill whistle to signal the start of the race.

Forty minutes later Gary crossed the finish line, panting, hands on hips, then looked around to see who was coming in second. It was a minute before anyone else appeared. He grinned. Somewhere in his head he could still hear Conflict's *Mental Mania*.

CHAPTER 1

1990 British Championship race 1
Edale Skyline Race, 25th March 1990
21 miles, 4500ft climb

"If you're young and talented, it's like you have wings."
— Haruki Murakami,
What I Talk About When I Talk About Running

Gary's van stuttered to a halt in a makeshift car park – a loaned farmer's field – on the edge of Edale village. A handful of people tumbled out, stiff, half-sick, stretching. More than a handful. Too many bodies to be squeezed into an ex-Post Office Escort estate along with their badly-packed kitbags and packed lunches and flasks and a grumpy Alsatian dog called Sheba. What was left of the winter's snow was slowly creeping back up north and the sky was a surprisingly clear blue. Surprising because this place, Edale – or, at least, the skyline of the surrounding hills – was known for its grizzled and biting cold, with a wind that roared across the Pennines on its way from Manchester to Sheffield. Over much of the upland ridges there were black peat bogs, huge sticky holes waiting to suck unprepared runners into the ground. Edale itself sat at the foot of these Pennine hills, a tiny village with a pub, a general store, a train station, a church – the Holy and Undivided Trinity Church – and the smallest primary school you're ever likely to see. It was the setting-off point for the Pennine Way long-distance path and the start and finish of the annual Edale Skyline fell race, a 21-mile slog that traced a huge circle around the surrounding hills.

For Gary, and for the few hundred fell runners gathering there early that day, the Skyline race was well-known as the classic early-season test of a winter's training. Not that the races had a winter break or anything; organised freezing scrambles carried on regardless through the winter months, albeit with a stricter insistence on full-body cover. In 1990 – when shorts were *really* short and only one company, Walsh, was making studded fell running shoes – runners' thermal body-covering had branched out from the regulation dull blue Helly Hansen Lifa (basically a thin wooly jumper) and Ron Hill Tracksters (tapered jogging bottoms that grew increasingly heavy in rain and mud) into a new explosion of multicoloured nylon. Now it was all candy-striped tights, yellow-and-purple rain jackets, Union Jack bobble-hats. This gathering of around 350 early-morning runners were Jackson Pollocked against the natural green-and-grey of the winter Pennine landscape, gathering slowly in the start field at the foot of the gentle river – Grinds Brook, what a gloriously apt name – that ran through Edale village. Heavy breathing, coughing, laughing, spitting, clapping, joking.

"A'right Gary. Another season, eh? Haven't seen you since, when was it?"

"Winter Hill race probably. Or Rombald's Moor. Nice haircut by the way. What happened to the mullet?"

"It was slowing me down. I blame it for every time you beat me last year."

"Well here's a little tip, you won't beat me with that moustache. My New Year's resolution, never to be beaten by anyone looking like Freddie Mercury."

This year the race would take on the extra significance of being the first in the 1990 Championship series, one of six races scattered across Britain's mountains and including the classic Snowdon and

Ben Nevis races, that would run until September. For those runners competing at the sharp end of the sport, the men and women looking around and nervously eyeing up the competition, those whose winters had been measured in training runs, here was where the season began.

Whether Gary was taking the race, the season and the Championship seriously or not was anybody's guess. Judging by the amount of good winter training he'd put in – twice-daily runs, track sessions on Mondays up at the old 440-yard cinder track at Weetwood, hill reps at Otley Chevin on Wednesdays, club run on Thursdays – you'd say he was focussed, fit, prepared, even. Judging by the amount of cider he'd drunk the previous day at Bradford's 1 in 12 Club, jumping up and down to a series of local punk bands –

Sore Throat
Biohazard
Disaster
No Way Out
Feeding for Two

– you'd say he was approaching the season in the same distracted and dispassionate way he approached life. Teachers would call it half-arsed, as if it was about lack of effort, which wasn't true at all. It was just that Gary sometimes enjoyed throwing himself into things, and sometimes those things didn't make sense, but he threw himself into them anyway; and sometimes he liked to walk away from things (girlfriends, fights, races) even when *those* things didn't make sense either.

The route of the Edale Skyline race covered classic northern-English fell-running terrain. A stiff, steep climb to a summit; long and undulating lines traced over moorland, sometimes on paths and sometimes with a compass and map; lots of rough tracks, sheep trods and peat hags; and finally a steep and rocky descent that piled down to walled fields and a lung-bursting race to finish where it started. There were times when the race was run with the tops in heavy cloud, obliterating the skyline, when the miles of open moorland on the run across to Brown Knoll were typified by runners desperately trying to follow the person in front who might be good with a compass (or might not. But sometimes any other human being will do). And there were times when the wind was so strong that the run across the exposed ridge on Mam Tor was a battle to stay upright; when the footpath up on the edge of the Kinder Plateau itself appeared to turn into one knee-deep, energy-sapping bog. All of this goes some way to explaining why the race was regarded as a classic.

There was a much more practical explanation for why Edale itself was regarded as the southern pivot of the Pennines – it had a train station. The line linked to both Manchester and Sheffield and was completed in 1894, at the fag-end of the Industrial Revolution, when both cities were notorious for cramped, unsanitary housing and smoke-belching factories and mills. Directly between these cotton and steel heavyweights rose the Peak District, described by Daniel Defoe as "the most desolate, wild and abandoned country in all England." Desolation and wildness would have been inviting to the armies of 19th-century mill workers desperate for space and peace on their one day off work. Too bad then that much of the Peaks, including the vast areas of upland above Edale, had a long history of being closed off to the general public. Twentieth-century landowners, whose families had been granted ownership a century or two earlier via the Parliamentary Enclosures Act, now kept it fenced and patrolled by gamekeepers, using it mainly for grouse-shooting. Several Bills calling for greater access to open land were put to Parliament between 1884 and 1926, and all were defeated.

By 1932 a head of steam had built up across various ramblers' and walkers' associations to the point where the suitably bolshy and energetic Manchester branch of the British Workers' Sports Federation

– including in its ranks many young communists – decided to take matters into their own hands. The now-legendary mass trespass on Kinder Scout (Roy Hattersley called it "the most successful direct action in British history"), when five ramblers were arrested and jailed for joining the gathering of 400 walkers intent on having a day out on Kinder, opened the floodgates to ever-increasing trespasses and the eventual acknowledgement that the tide had turned. The next few decades would be marked by a rapidly-growing demand for the right to roam. Edale was chosen by its inspired originator Tom Stephenson in 1935 as the start of the first long-distance footpath in the country, marking the opening of the land. It took Stephenson 30 years to negotiate the legal right of way for the footpath – historian Ann Holt called the access issue "an apparently simple idea with revolutionary implications", while Stephenson's close friend Sylvia Franks put it more bluntly: "the landowners didn't want the hoi polloi walking on their land, that was the top and bottom of it."

The start of the 1990 Edale Skyline race was one such gathering of the hoi polloi. Here were runners of all shapes and sizes in their multicoloured kit and peat-stained socks and damp, muddy studded shoes, laughing and swearing and checking and re-checking and re-re-checking their bumbags. Everyone was required to carry full body cover (including hat and gloves), along with a map, a compass, a whistle and emergency food. The food was usually either a small slab of Kendal Mint Cake or a Mars bar. Getting around a race like this meant re-fuelling somewhere along the way, which meant stopping off at a garage en route to the race and stocking up on chocolate. Water was drunk from streams with cupped hands – some more sophisticated long-distance fell and mountain runners brought small plastic bags to fill up at river-crossings and drink on the run, so as not to waste any time.

Gary was here with a motley assortment of runners in the maroon-and-gold colours of Pudsey & Bramley AC. They were nominally an athletics club, but more accurately a gang. Any pretentions towards being seasoned athletes seemed far-fetched as they all tumbled shambolically out of the van, these six or seven runners who'd spent a cramped morning squeezed into the back of a tiny vehicle with no seats and no windows, most of them now complaining of either travel sickness or of having had Sheba repeatedly lolling onto their lap on the drive down to Edale. They shook themselves off, traded insults for a few minutes and then dug out vests and shorts, checking their kit, fiddling with safety pins and shoelaces and looking around them at the skyline they'd be racing along. Registration for the race was in the scout hut next to the village car park. The hut was a pre-fabricated single room; it didn't need a toilet because there was an adjacent public loo in the car park, a red-brick box furnished with urine-stained aluminium. The hut was teeming with runners and, even before the race had started, it reeked of sweat – or rather, it was the smell that running clothes take on when they've been repeatedly sweated into, an odour born of soil, effort, perspiration, fear and hundreds of miles stuffed into kitbags, a smell that no known washing detergent can eradicate.

Race organisers and helpers, some still wearing their coats and hats, arranged themselves behind wooden trestle tables in a perfectly coordinated line that began with Name & Club Registration, followed by a shuffle through Payment (it was £2.50 to enter), Race Number Allocation, and finally a scruffy cardboard box full of blank and open brown envelopes. Runners dropped their 20p pieces into the envelope to cover postage and scribbled their name and address on the front. A week from now they'd get this same envelope through their letterbox with the full results of the race typed out and photocopied along with a paragraph of thank-yous from the organiser. The entire registration process was a triumph of do-it-yourself unfussiness, and it worked perfectly well.

This was part of fell running's attraction: several hundred people turning up in the middle of nowhere, competing and organising with minimum intervention from bureaucratic officialdom. The national committee for the Fell Runners Association was made up of fell runners who practised a fairly hands-off approach, even though this was a time of change within the sport – with the legalities of insurance, access and permissions and the whole amateur vs professional debate vying to get in the way of a relatively uncluttered sport.

Other clubs turning up in Edale came from all over Britain. There were the big, well-organised clubs like Lancashire's Clayton Harriers and Bingley Harriers from Yorkshire, the Lake District mountain specialists from Ambleside and Keswick and contenders from Wales and Scotland. Gary's Pudsey & Bramley club, based in the jumble of red brick and ring road between Leeds and Bradford, was the tiniest of clubs whose membership was almost completely focussed on fell running. Even cross-country races were looked down upon – they were part of a winter training schedule, but (sniff), they were *flat*. The club's numbers swelled as more cars arrived and their distinctive club colours were fished out of carrier bags and holdalls. Gary was relaxed, wearing a notably untroubled expression. Not that this was unusual – Gary's general emotional setting was happy-go-lucky, a disorganised nonchalance that came with a quick smile and a put-down. His amiable cockiness fell some distance short of arrogance, and any self-confidence he had was balanced by a healthy acceptance of failure – it wasn't that he didn't want to win, but that he didn't spend time mentally beating himself up if he didn't. It was far too early in the season for him to be thinking about the Championship, and he refused to plan further than a couple of months ahead; in fact, most of the time he found it difficult to plan into next week. It was an attitude that suited both his running and his lifestyle – he'd only just turned 23 and he was having the time of his life switching between punk rock gigs and mountain races. There was, he'd decided, no need to overthink it all; so many young people seemed to spend their youth wanting and trying to get older. Inviting responsibility and attachments, maturity and wisdom … not Gary. Like J.D. Salinger's anti-hero in *Catcher in the Rye*, he delighted in the immediate here-and-now-ness of being young: "How do you know what you're going to do till you do it? The answer is, you don't."

The race organiser, in cream overcoat and bobble hat and with a whistle strung around his neck, raised his voice to address the chattering bunch. He'd been told several times that he could use the Edale Scouts megaphone but he thought it needlessly official to be barking out instructions, such as they were, through a loudhailer. Bit fancy.

"Right. Everybody! EVERYBODY!"

A vague version of a hush fell, like an errant school assembly.

"Thanks for coming. Hope you've all got your kit. Hand your tags in to the checkpoint marshals. Bloody freezing innit? Right, on your marks –"

He stood back, seeing the front few rows of runners crouching, heads down.

"– oh, one more thing."

A muttered collective groan.

"Hot pie and peas at the hut when you've finished, and cakes and such in aid of the local village hall."

And with that he blew his whistle and the runners headed off, up the start field that was too steep for a stampede, towards an open gate and onto the fell proper, straight into a steep climb.

Gary had raced this landscape several times before, and liked it in amongst these Peak District hills. It suited him, the rough ground and the bogs, the steep final descent and the tussocky moors. One thing he thrived on, though, was missing today – harsh weather. It was often the rain, snow or wind that separated the good athletes, with their training plans and sensible diets, their carbo-loading and their stopwatches, from the natural fell runners. A generalisation, admittedly, but with more and more emphasis being placed on the international mountain running scene – and its attendant prize-money and lucrative race invitations – there was a slowly emerging shift in the culture of fell running. Since 1985 the advent of the World Mountain Running Trophy had introduced elite British fell runners to worldwide events; Keswick hosted the 1988 edition of the Trophy. This and various other continental mountain races had become notable summer fixtures for athletes being offered travel costs and free accommodation to compete. 'Pure' fell runners were having to decide whether they wanted their love of fell racing – with its attendant injury risks and habitual over-racing – to jeopardise their chances of international competition ("Yes, I do over-race," admitted Gary in an interview with a local newspaper, "but I love it.").

What Gary enjoyed was the rough stuff, the unexpected, the obstacles that constituted the difference between fell running and trail running: ankle-turning ditches, lashing rain, on-the-hoof navigation, clawing slutch, low visibility. Proper British conditions – the cloud and puddles that suited the landscape. Some of Gary's first races, run as a junior under BOFRA rules, featured wall-climbs, river-crossings and rock scrambles. Kilnsey Show's fell race, notorious within the sport, was one such short, sharp classic – it descended via a short but sheer rock-funnel-drop that zigzagged between overhanging trees and a limestone wall. Reaching the finish with battered and scraped legs was some sort of minor blood ritual there. Gary loved the short and brutal Kilnsey race, embracing it as the antithesis of the neat and regimented against-the-clock track racing he had grown bored of as a junior athlete.

Small pity, then, that 1990's Edale Skyline Race was blessed with a crisp but clear-blue-sky morning, most of the runners opting for vests and shorts. The race favourites, chatting and smiling up at the front of the gathering bunch of runners in the start field, included the three-times British Fell Running Champion Colin Donnelly of Welsh club Eryri, stocky local lad Andy Trigg, the slight and blue-shirted Shaun Livesey of Rossendale and Ambleside's Keith Anderson, winner of the previous year's Edale Skyline Race. It was Anderson who started as favourite, despite the presence of Donnelly. Three years earlier Keith Anderson had been a thirty-year-old, overweight, 20-a-day smoker who decided he needed to get healthy. His fitness regime had led him to the hills and to some remarkable victories, and he was known as an incredible descender. Despite doing a lot of his training on an indoor treadmill, he could hurtle down a rock-strewn mountainside faster than any other fell runner. Favourite among the women aiming to win the year's Championship was Trish Calder of Edinburgh, improving and seemingly unbeatable.

It was no surprise that as soon as the runners had begun to string out from the start field, Keith Anderson was at the front – runners snaking behind him up the first stiff climb towards the skyline. The first rough ascent led up, up, up straight away towards the peaty hilltop, indistinct and meandering as it crested the skyline and headed for the forest wall at the eastern edge of the Kinder Plateau. The runners, having scrambled and grovelled to the high and open plateau, began to spread out and splinter, their slithering line stretching and breaking. From here there was a three-mile section of fast moor-top running, along the wall side and towards the descent to the road crossing just north of Hope village. The ten or twenty leading contenders formed a Morse code dot-dash-dot of clusters and solo runners, gaps appearing and closing between them. Gary was running alongside Shaun Livesey, around fifty metres behind Keith Anderson in the lead, and behind them the field stretched back and out of sight, an ever-stretching thread of muddied, panting runners.

Shaun Livesey was already a fell running legend. He was short and smiley with a reputation for high-mileage training, an evergreen on the fell running scene who, despite running for England in international competition, often missed out in the Championships due to injury and illness. He was popular, too – he typified a sport that refused the idea of elites, always willing to joke and natter before the race began. In fact, he was, like Gary, a runner who would chat during a race, striking up discussions about who might be ahead or behind, whether it was the right time to put in an effort, wondering where there might be water, discussing route choices. This easy chat that ran between many of the top runners – even during important Championship races – was another example of the way fell running somehow refused to pander to ego and expertise. Yes, some runners were highly-trained and serious about the sport. But on the start line there was an egalitarianism that refused professional sport's ruthless star-system.

As Anderson hit the road crossing at Hope village he knew he had a good lead; he pressed on. Behind him, Devine and Livesey were separated from the masses of runners behind them, shoulder-to-shoulder and running easily. The next section, the stiff climb up to Lose Hill, took the runners off the road and onto grassy tracks. It was here that Shaun and Gary realised that they could no longer see Keith in front of them – he'd disappeared, missing the turning leading onto the fells after the road crossing and carrying on along the tarmac back towards Edale village. By the time Keith had realised his mistake and doubled back to rejoin the race, Gary and Shaun were sharing jokes about where Anderson might have disappeared to. As they quick-stepped up the long climb, Shaun suggested that, with the harsh navigation of the western end of the race yet to come – the roughest of semi-circles across peat hags, natural drainage ditches and sheep-trods – he and Gary might stick together. Safety in numbers. Gary thought about it for ten seconds before grinning and putting in an effort that took him clear of Livesey. It wasn't an arrogant or selfish move; more an act of self-preservation. Shaun was at his best on the long races, and knew if he could navigate himself around the trickier sections of the route (or jump behind someone else's better route finding) without getting hopelessly lost, he might have a good chance of winning overall.

Gary had an instinct for navigation. He wasn't sure where it had come from – perhaps from years of running on the fells as a teenager – but he had an in-built compass that belied his reputation as a punk; chaotic, rebellious and gloriously directionless. If an opportunity came up to try a different, unexplored route during a race, he'd take it. Everyone else is going that way … well what about this way? Let's try it and see. Anything in the name of adventure, of seeing what happens. With Keith Anderson now some way behind it fell to Gary to plough on alone up to the exposed summit of Mam Tor and on towards the hellish peat-bog moonscape that typified the second third of the route – no paths, no walls or fences, and usually nothing to aim for but low cloud and a compass bearing; nothing but the left-right-left-right rhythm of your studded shoes, the in-out-in-out beat of your breath.

Gary, like most runners, often ran with a tune in his head, a tune to fit the rhythm of running, the default timing of his feet. Cultural theorists realised long ago that the northern hemisphere's supposed 'natural' 4/4 doesn't originate in the womb (rocking along with mother's walking) but from our exposure to music; small children in the Balkans or in Africa will happily clap along to complex 7/8 rhythms. Punk rock is defiantly 4/4. When the Ramones played their first concert in London in 1976 they effectively swept away any pretensions of rhythmic complexity and flicked a V-sign at a generation of musicians meddling with that basic beat. Hey ho, let's go, hey, ho, let's go. One foot in front of the other, back to basics. The Amebix were a four-piece punk band from Devon whose first, four-track EP *Who's the Enemy* was released in 1982. The band comprised The Baron, Stig, Virus and Norman and their self-styled musical genre was 'crustcore'. They were proudly dirtier, uglier, faster and louder than any other band, their music a full-throated guttural yell. Melody wasn't a word in the Amebix dictionary. Gary loved them. One of the songs from the EP was 'No Gods, No Masters', a raging stomp that had only three lines of lyrics:

Your god is your chains
Reject your god, reject the system
Do you really want your freedom?

Gary could run all day to that song. It fitted with his outlook and it fitted with the landscape – up on these moors, nothing but peat bogs and sky, no rules, no orders, no bosses, just the 1,2,3,4 punk rock rhythm that connected through his fell running shoes to the green and brown earth. Down below, somewhere in the valley, there was the everyday thrum of life, Give Way signs and butcher's shops, churches and front lawns, tea rooms and petrol stations. Up here there was only flesh, blood, earth and sky, all in complete synchronicity. Gary had the Amebix's 'No Gods, No Masters' slogan tattooed on his left arm, big and blotchy, the words spelled out in bones along with an image of a body hanging limply from a cross. Anyone looking for an answer to the lyric *'Do you really want your freedom?'* might start up there on the heavy slog between Lord's Seat and Brown Knoll, two of the race's checkpoints at the western edge of the Edale valley. The ground around the skyline, 2,000 feet up, is basically a mixture of peat and millstone grit, a porous rock that absorbs water. The land shifts from year to year depending on the rainfall; springs appear and disappear; narrow river valleys come and go according to the amount of frost and sun. It was on this stretch of the route, with Shaun Livesey sticking doggedly to Gary's route across the moor, that the race could be won or lost – fifteen miles covered and the battle becoming attritional, a measure not just of fitness and speed but of dogged persistence and will. As the pair approached the top of Jacob's Ladder, the valley sweeping down to their right, Shaun joined Gary and then gradually moved ahead, while just behind them, quietly and with an athlete's sense of when to strike, Colin Donnelly drew closer with each mud-clawing step.

Colin Donnelly was in his prime as a mountain runner, a brilliant Glaswegian athlete who'd already won the British Championship three times along with victories at Ben Nevis and Snowdon. Dark-haired and taciturn, he typified the fell running ethos – he excelled at the sport he loved and was never happier than when he was tackling an extreme mountain run. As a 20-year-old he'd run unaccompanied for eleven days covering 130 summits of the Southern Uplands of Scotland, coast-to-coast from the Moorfoots to the Cheviots, a distance of 380 miles with 82,000 feet of ascent. In short, the man was an animal – tough, determined and incredibly focussed, his love of fell running evident in his joyful assertion that, "If you want to run you just go out there any time of the day. The equipment's absolutely minimal and there's a fantastic sense of freedom. The world's your oyster."

As the race leaders rounded the north-western edge of the skyline and joined the footpath towards Grindslow Knoll, Donnelly gradually overtook a tiring Gary and Shaun and step by step by step pulled away on the long descent from Ringing Roger – a rocky outcrop that stands high above the sweeping valley – down to the finish and to victory. Trish Calder, meanwhile, had started the season in style, coasting clear of Cheryl Cook and breaking the previous Edale women's course record by six minutes.

Here was Donnelly laying down a marker for another year of domination on the fells. Unlike Gary, he always had a plan, and the main thrust of the plan was simply *coming first*. He was a competitor, and the one thing he understood was the will to win. Shaun Livesey came in second, careering off the lower slopes a minute later, and Gary followed in third place, knackered but grinning. Keith Anderson was fourth, leading in a string of seasoned mountain runners who would all play some part in the year's Championship. The 1932 Kinder

Trespassers would have loved it – a fieldful of mud-spattered folk finding an excuse to reclaim the hills around them, circumscribing a route that was open and free, the world their oyster. Gary, his bleached hair showing no remains of the previous year's pink dye, ambled back to his yellow van and woke up the sleeping Sheba. He'd been gone for a little over two-and-a-half hours, and in that short time he'd been to the edge of the world and back. He pulled on a tatty tracksuit top and headed for the pub.

CHAPTER 2

"No one can tell what goes on in between the person you were and the person you become. No one can chart that blue and lonely section of hell. There are no maps of the change. You just come out the other side. Or you don't."

— Stephen King

1981 was a hell of a year for Margaret Thatcher's Conservative government, custodians of the country as unemployment reached a record three million (the worst figures since the 1930s). The year saw industrial disputes, mass marches and protests against a backdrop of IRA hunger strikes and mainland bombings. Manufacturing plants were closing across the country and being replaced by 'Enterprise Zones', out-of-town, pre-fabbed, windowless industrial hangars. Enoch Powell was banging on about immigration, again, and to spice up the summer Britain saw a series of ongoing inner-city riots that lit up:

London
Liverpool
Manchester
Birmingham
Sheffield
Nottingham
Wolverhampton
Newcastle

Hull

... and Leeds.

Meanwhile, Charles and Di got married, Bucks Fizz won the Eurovision Song Contest and Gary Devine finished ninth in the English Schools Cross Country race. He was a round-collared 15-year-old schoolboy at St Mary's Catholic School in Menston, a thirty-minute jog up the road from his home in Ilkley, and his main concerns were the lunchtime cross-country runs under the watchful eye of wiry and athletic PE teacher Terry Lonergan. Terry's life in running began with being unable to reach the final of his school's Under-12s 100-yard dash. He quickly worked out that the longer the distance, the better he ran. By the age of 14 he was invited to join Sale Harriers, excelling in cross-country and steeplechase racing, and started at St Mary's after moving over to attend college in Yorkshire. Terry loved his running. He was obsessed. Teaching PE was alright, he could turn up in his tracksuit instead of a shirt and tie and he ruled the fiefdom of the school gym, as well as enjoying long holidays with no marking and bourbon biscuits and strong tea in the smoky staffroom every break. But running was his passion, something he excelled at, something he could teach that wasn't ex-army exercise drills and lining up the kids to vault a scuffed wooden horse. Terry knew that in amongst the disinterested kids, the kids with half a kit, the kids who didn't give a shit about sport, the kids with the rugby dads who were forced to try out as scrum-halfs and fly-halfs and loosehead props and blind-side flankers and open-side flankers, somewhere in the melee of forgotten gym kit and goosebumped legs there were some kids who just needed pushing and pulling into shape and they'd learn to love running, too.

The school's headmaster, on the other hand, saw sport merely as a distraction from the pursuit of academic excellence. Despite the school being a comprehensive, he liked to imagine it was a grammar school, and he made his disdain for both arts and sports subjects clear.

Much to his displeasure he was forced to accept that the school's sitting Parish Priest, who had inherited the job of interviewing prospective teachers for the school, didn't share his sneering antipathy towards running, tackling, vaulting, leaping, bowling, throwing, catching and any other diversion from the job of getting an annual handful of students to Oxbridge.

"Remind me, who is this new chap in the jogging bottoms?"

"He's the new games teacher, and his name is Mr. Lonergan."

"Lonergan? Sounds foreign."

"Yes. He's from Manchester."

"Oh dear."

"He's an exceptional teacher. Very inspirational."

"Really? I've seen him waving his arms around and heard him blowing his whistle and very little else."

"Well … he's already got a lot of the pupils motivated through his physical education classes."

"Really? All I see is a lot of huffing and puffing. In the words of Groucho Marx, 'He may look like an idiot and talk like an idiot but don't let that fool you. He really is an idiot.'"

Every September, at the start of the school year, Terry would send the new classes on a couple of laps of the football pitches, no pressure, in your own time, just to warm up. Only it wasn't to warm up, it was so he could pick out the competitive ones who made an effort, who wanted to win, but it was also so he could single out the smokers who dawdled and pretended they were injured, who thought it was uncool to look like you were trying. The competitive kids were easy, but he needed the smokers and the dawdlers because they were a challenge, and because every year he'd get a couple of them up with the competitive lot, and they'd be dead chuffed and they'd stop smoking and he'd turn their lives around. He knew that's what running could do, and he loved it.

Lunchtimes most days, before school dinners had stopped being served and while the other teachers were mixing up huge mugs of Nescafe in the staffroom and moaning about some lad in year nine who'd threatened to punch the school caretaker, Terry would gather a pack of kids and head off for a 40-minute cross-country run that took them out of the back gates and up the road, up to the paths and trails and cut-throughs across local farmland towards the Chevin hill, with his crocodile of lads and lasses slipping around in the mud behind him. Terry knew that every year there'd be one or two runners who he'd be able to turn into competitive athletes, club runners, winners even.

Gary turned up at St Mary's as an eleven-year-old and straight away joined Terry's lunchtime group – he was already running regularly with his dad Hughie, already beating his mates and already racing sporadically in local professional junior fell races. Even as a young teenager Gary could disappear with the family dogs up onto Ilkley Moor and be out for an hour, two hours, calling the dogs to heel as the paths took him high up above the reservoirs and the stony track to the Swastika Stone, up along the century-old drystone walls and over the stiles and gates that marked the boundaries between open land and farm land. Gary's dad had encouraged him to run in the junior race at the annual professional Ilkley Moor Fell Race: Hughie knew, all the dads knew, that the first five runners won a bit of cash stuffed into a brown paper envelope. Meeting up with Terry Lonergan, though, was something else – Gary's irregular and unstructured running became an everyday part of his life, and finding himself part of a school group that ran almost every day meant that he started taking his running more seriously, not least because it made him realise that he was good. Terry knew it, too. This scruffy lad with the German-helmet haircut, the quiet lad with the grin, he could go far, he could make it at regional level, county level, national level. He didn't say much, and he looked like he wasn't paying attention, and he looked like he didn't care, but once he was running you could see that he was a natural.

After one of his Wednesday lunchtime runs, Terry asked Gary to stay behind for a few minutes while the rest went back to get changed. He asked him how things were at home, about what he wanted to do with his life, asked him about ambition, about running, about joining a proper club. Gary knew what he meant. For the past couple of years, he'd had various people watching him doing well in the little Sunday professional races around the Dales, the fast up-and-down races over in the tucked-away towns and villages at Cracoe and Skipton and Addingham. Various people who'd have a quiet word after the race to tell him he maybe should be training with a club, taking it seriously. Gary would feign interest, mutter an embarrassed thank you, and quietly forget about it. He didn't fancy taking it seriously. He was enjoying himself. Gary had found a perfect way to be away from any simmering tensions between his mum and dad by slipping on some training shoes and heading off to the fields to run. It was easy out there – just him and the whole of Ilkley Moor, no arguments, no homework, no older sister or kid brother.

Somehow though it was different when Terry talked to him. Because Terry knew, didn't he? He knew this was more than getting better by joining a club, more than improving by competing more – this was about learning to love running for its own sake, turning it into a part of your life, something that would stick around for as long as he had legs to move and a world to explore. What Gary was scared of, more than anything, was losing his love of the sport by taking it too seriously, by making it all about personal bests and training schedules, ironed club vests and clean spikes, clipboards and stopwatches. But this was Terry, and Terry was a runner himself, Terry had won races, proper races that got reported in the *Yorkshire Post*, and Terry knew.

Here was the confusing conundrum at the heart of running – the part of it that was existential freedom and escape, a singular, windblown adventure of discovery; and the part of it that was rigour, training, discipline, patience and consistency. For any young teenager, the second option wouldn't look too inviting. For Gary, it looked and felt alien to the running he'd been enjoying, the running he'd learned by simply being out on the moors with the dogs at his heels. Terry knew better than to suggest training schedules, but he also knew that throwing some method and practice into the mix would make Gary a better runner.

Hughie Devine's home, meanwhile, was an exercise in fun and unpredictability with a reputation as a gathering place for wider friends and family. Parents, children and various dogs came and went along with a stream of passing visitors. Every Sunday, from spring to autumn, there was an all-day congregation of aunts, uncles, cousins, mates and neighbours, a crowd that functioned around a Sunday roast and plenty of bottled ale. The kids would populate the basement, nipping in and out of the kitchen for food, taking the dogs out for walks and generally messing around. Of all the kids, Gary was the quiet, unassuming but incredibly confident lad who had the ability to cause trouble without worrying about the consequences (and without worrying about getting caught). He had a reputation for calmness in the middle of chaos, and Gary's second cousin Jan – awkward, funny, wide-eyed Jan with his patch-pocket shirts and manic laugh – would remind everyone about the time he, Bradley and Gary found themselves as eight- and nine-year-olds being swept out to sea off the French coast in an inflatable dinghy, unable to fight the tide. Hughie had tried to swim out to reach them but couldn't make it. As Bradley and Jan panicked and shouted for help, and even as some French canoeists heroically came to their rescue, Gary had remained serenely, gently, smilingly placid.

It was sometime during one of these Sunday throngs in early 1981 that Jan, crucially a year or two older, sassier and louder than the Devine brothers, turned up with his hair dyed bright green and wearing bondage trousers and a torn T-shirt.

Boom!

Gary was gobsmacked. As a teenager, Gary's dad had been in a skiffle band himself, and Jan's dad and mum had been teddy boy and teddy girl. Still, this was different – it seemed to Gary that Jan was making a point, staking a claim for himself. It was his enthusiastic, bubbly older cousin saying "Look at me! I'm not like you!" Hughie asked Jan why he'd dyed his hair, and Jan had replied, simply: "I'm a punk now." Gary was shocked and impressed. Jan was such a lovely lad, so friendly and funny, and here he was in a pair of trousers full of buckles and straps, straps where there was no need for straps, zips where there was no need for zips. It didn't make sense; but the senselessness was somehow compelling. When everyone had gone home, and with Hughie fast asleep in an armchair in front of the TV still clutching a bottle of stout, Gary quizzed his younger brother Bradley about what they'd just witnessed. Gary was somehow hoping for an explanation, some reasoning –

"What did you make of our Jan?"

"Eh?"

"Jan. What's going on there?"

Bradley didn't take his eyes away from the telly: it was BBC One's Sunday film, *Carry On Constable,* the one where a group of new recruits try to shake up a small police force headed up by Sid James. Fat chance.

"I mean all those straps and stuff. And his hair."

"Dunno."

"What did you think though?"

"Weird."

That was all. Gary realised he wasn't going to get anything else out of Bradley so he went off through the kitchen to the back door that squeaked on its hinges and pulled on his running shoes, heading out along the steep streets up towards the moor and wondering where and when and why and how Jan had learned to dye his hair. Bright green, like Kermit off *Sesame Street*, like one of the Queen Mother's hats, like the Riddler or the Jolly Green Giant. And short. Not covering his ears. How would that feel? How would that look? Would anyone care? (Of course they would, and that was the point.)

At school, Terry Lonergan didn't let up on encouraging some of his lunchtime runners – especially Gary – to start training seriously, which meant somehow getting them over to the other side of Ilkley and Baildon moors every Tuesday and Thursday evening to train with Bingley Harriers at Nab Wood. At first Lonergan would ferry them over in his old Ford estate car but more pupils wanted to get involved. Terry's plan to use the school's minibus was thwarted when the headmaster – seeing the popularity of the scheme – promptly sold it. The problem was solved when local coach and enthusiast Gordon Agar – a jolly-looking type who sported an Amish beard – offered to make the regular trip over the hill with his own minibus, filling it full of teenagers. At Bingley they had a 400-metre track, with spotlights and hurdles and a sandpit for the steeplechase and a place for everything and everything in its place. There were qualified coaches who ran the sessions, high-visibility vests in winter, and all of it planned and organised. Gary was worried about losing his evenings up on the hill with the dogs, his rides out with his dad to tackle the professional races, his easy weekend runs out in the Dales. But both Terry and Gordon's nagging were persuasive, and flattering, and Gary knew that if he wanted his running to go further, he'd need to change the routines he loved, run outside his comfort zone. Gary finally agreed to link up with the training sessions at Bingley Harriers.

Sometime in early spring, and just before the Easter school holidays, Gary was talking to his mate Richard Pallister – one of Terry Lonergan's lunchtime runners – in the school hall, feet up on the chair in front of him and tie-knot slipped down just that bit further than school rules allowed. Richard, tall and good-looking in a straight-nosed, dark-eyed, perfectly-proportioned film-star kind of way, was two years older than Gary, but they shared a passion for anything athletic. Both were good at gymnastics, football, field sports

and running. Neither had much interest in the school's preferred sport, rugby union, joking that it was just the fat lads charging into each other in the mud.

Richard's mate John was, like Richard, older than Gary but loudly dismissive of anyone who was involved in any form of sport. He wrote angry poems for the school magazine and drew scurrilous (but perfectly accurate) cartoons of the teachers, especially the teachers who swaggered and smoked and drove Ford Cortinas and threw chalk at kids' heads. John constantly tried to test how far he could undermine the school uniform before being sent to detention, which was at least once a week. Today, as he sauntered past he was, Gary noted, wearing bright pink socks. That'll be a detention tonight, then. John gave Richard a cursory nod and Richard called him over.

"What you got there, John?"

"An LP. Just got it back off Ady."

"Let's have a look."

"You won't like it. Fucking extreme."

"I might."

"You won't."

"Give it here."

John held out the album, its Germanic title lettering set against a black-and-white photograph that neither Richard nor Gary could make out. It said, 'Dead Kennedys' and it featured a highly-contrasted picture of a police car, which had been set alight and was burning.

"What is it?" asked Gary.

John let Gary grab hold of it, enjoying seeing the two lads baffled.

"It's the best record ever made, that's what it is."

Gary flipped it over. On the reverse sleeve, against a pale cream background, there was a publicity shot of a jazz or swing band, a band with brass instruments, a band with a woman wearing a trouser suit, a band where all the men had bow ties and Brylcreemed hair and sensible shoes. Above the band were the words, FRESH FRUIT FOR

ROTTING VEGETABLES.

It made no sense.

Gary didn't care about music. Radio One – which everyone seemed to listen to, and know about, and talk about, was just a background blur of meaningless noise, irrelevant and insipid. It was Shakin' Stevens singing 'This Ole House', it was Phil Collins singing 'In the Air Tonight'. It was wallpaper. Sometimes when he ran he'd have some annoying pop song or children's rhyme going around his head in rhythm with his striding feet, and it would drive him half-mad trying to get rid of it. And his older sister Lynne, she'd told him the best way to get rid of an annoying song that's in your head is to think of another song, something you like, and force it to replace the annoying one. Only Gary could never think of a song he liked. Sometimes he'd try to replace the annoying song with one of his dad's old country songs that he'd sing in the bathroom like, 'I Shot a Man in Reno' or 'Trailer for Sale or Rent' or 'Someone Left the Cake Out in the Rain', but then he'd start to hate those, too.

John was waiting for Gary to give him his record back. "It's punk," he declared. "Dead Kennedys. They're American. John Peel plays them."

Gary had no idea who John Peel was. Richard gave up on the record sleeve with its trouser suits and burning cop cars and started to talk to John about something that had happened to someone from their class and wasn't it funny and they both laughed, but Gary didn't laugh because he was still scanning the back sleeve of the Dead Kennedys album and looking at the titles and the names of the people in the band and he was remembering his cousin Jan standing there with his green hair saying, "I'm a punk now." And whatever it all meant (and he had little clue what it all meant), Gary couldn't stop looking at the strange sleeve, turning it over to look at the cover, turning it back again to the bow ties and the sensible shoes.

"Can I borrow it?"

John stopped talking to Richard and Richard turned to look at Gary. Since neither of them had ever seen Gary express any interest in music, at all, ever, not even once, this sounded peculiar and somehow unreasonable. Like he hadn't earned the right to ask to borrow it. You had to know stuff, talk about stuff, show people you were part of the club.

"Er ... I'm not sure. I've only just got it back."

"Go on, just for tonight. Our Bradley can tape it and I'll bring it back tomorrow."

*

Dead Kennedys were formed in 1978 when guitarist East Bay Ray met up with vocalist Jello Biafra. The band's first single, 'California Uber Alles', along with their shocking name, marked them out as a band intending to upset the cultural apple cart. As well as being loud and fast they boasted clever, literate and ironic lyrics. On stage, Jello was pure theatre, peppering the songs with characters, mimicking and ridiculing those in power. That first album, not released in the UK until 1980, was two years old by the time Gary first heard it. Nevertheless, it immediately, directly and permanently changed the young boy's life. Listening to it at home, Gary found it impossible to describe what it was about the record that grabbed him so much. His previous disinterest in music, and especially in the stuff he'd heard on the radio, was based on a complete lack of any visceral, physical connection to it. Pop music didn't make him want to dance, or sing along, or watch *Top of the Pops*, or tune into the Sunday evening Radio One Chart Countdown, or buy those crappy magazines which were just collections of the lyrics to the week's top hits, music did nothing for him. The Dead Kennedys were different. This music was different. It swore, it raged and it refused to be tamed. It was an explosion going off – a mixture of melodic guitar lines cranked through overdrive and distortion pedals and a voice that warbled, cried and hollered through spittle and splutter.

The album's opening song, 'Kill the Poor' unknowingly alluded to Jonathan Swift's 1729 satire 'A Modest Proposal', an essay which offers eating destitute children as a simple solution to poverty. In Jello Biafra's lyrics, the twentieth-century solution is the atomic bomb:

The sun beams down on a brand new day
No more welfare tax to pay
Unsightly slums gone up in flashing light
Jobless millions whisked away
At last we have more room to play
All systems go to kill the poor tonight
Gonna kill kill kill kill kill the poor
Kill kill kill kill kill the poor
Kill kill kill kill kill the poor tonight

When Jello Biafra barked that full-throttle repeating chorus he was knowingly articulating something much more than loud music that annoyed your parents. Here, in a yelled three-minute howl of rage, was an invitation to a subculture that embraced an entire lifestyle: music, style and attitude. It embraced how you felt about the world, what you ate, how you lived, and it threw up a sense of wild, disorganised adventure.

The first band to sing about 'no future' were the Sex Pistols, half a decade earlier. Their song 'God Save the Queen' screamed, 'Where there's no future, how can there be sin?' and set a blueprint for punk, for a cultural movement that struck a balance between nihilism and social responsibility, between believing in self-destruction and believing in making the world a better place. A mad, confused set of ideas held together by a desire for excitement and change. Gary had missed the

Sex Pistols and the furore surrounding the first wave of punk, but now it had caught up with him, here in his house, first with Jan's zips and straps and now with Jello Biafra's 100mph sermonising.

This language of daring and confrontation couldn't have been further from the handbook text of the British athletics establishment in 1981. The Amateur Athletics Association and its Northern Counties administrative arm were still, in the main, old-fashioned, blazer-wearing traditionalists, bound up in rules and regulations, fighting a losing battle against the professionalisation of their amateur sport. Track and field differed from most sports in that it depended heavily on measurements and timings, and by its nature it had always needed an official holding a stopwatch or tape measure. It wasn't a sport that encouraged innovation or rule-bending – quite the opposite, it emphasised discipline, focus and meticulous preparation.

These two worlds – the screaming nihilism of punk, and the measured diligence of athletics – were about to have a big, dirty, no-holds-barred scrap in the grey scramble of Gary's head. It was a fight that, ultimately, both sides would win.

CHAPTER 3

1990 British Championship race 2
Pen-y-Fan Race, 7th April 1990
3.5 miles, 2000ft climb

"It's brutal but it doesn't go on for long."
— Pen-y-Fan race organiser

The 'Fan Dance' was, for years, an essential part of the British Army's combat fitness course, a forced march in the Brecon Beacons carrying full pack that counted towards every new recruit's selection for the Special Forces. Army-speak referred to the Fan Dance as a test of "physical fitness, mental robustness and determination" – in reality it was the army's way of seeing if they could break the weaker recruits, a way of filtering out the feeble. The 15-mile course's highest point, and the most daunting section of the Dance, was the summit of Pen-y-Fan, at just under 3,000 feet tall the highest British peak south of Snowdon.

In April 1990, 123 runners arrived at the foot of the mountain, ready for the season's second Championship race, a 3.5-mile lung-buster with one of fell racing's classic descents. The course was short enough for some of the runners to recce the route on the morning of the race, out along an old cart track and up to the summit skyline before a steep, hair-raising drop off the north edge of the ridge and a sprint all the way to the finish. The bunch of runners from Pudsey & Bramley did not, as usual, arrive in time to recce the route. Hughie's white works van ('Devine & Pearson. Builders') had trundled around the no-man's (and no-women's) land between Leeds and Bradford not long after sunrise, picking up various runners and their oversized kitbags and sardining them into the stifling, windowless back with Gary's drooling, claustrophobic, German Shepherd Sheba. The long journey down to the Brecon Beacons afforded them one piss stop and one piss stop only, that was the rule, stop your moaning, one stop, no matter how many times you sing "Does the driver want a wee-wee, 'cause we want a wee-wee too". More than one stop and they'd all have missed registration and the start of the race, which as far as most of the team knew was somewhere in Wales and featured a mountain.

Two weeks earlier, the phone rang in Hughie's kitchen, right in the middle of BBC's *Wogan on Ice*, a chat show special featuring ice dancers Jayne Torvill and Christopher Dean. Not that he cared much for ice dancing, but Wogan – Wogan was an institution, and by Hughie's slightly drunk early evening calculations, everybody in the country should be watching *Wogan on Ice*.

"Yes?"

"Dad."

"Oh. It's you. 'Course it is. Who else do I know who hasn't got a telly?"

"What?"

"Nowt. Go on."

"We've got a Championship race down in Wales."

"Wales? Whereabouts in Wales?"

"Erm – I'm not sure. Somewhere with mountains."

"Right. And you want to borrow my van."

"No, I want you to drive us all there."

"You cheeky bugger. You're not daft are you? When is it?"

"In a fortnight. Two weeks Saturday."

"Hmm. I'll have to check what's going on here."

"It starts and finishes at a pub."

"Eh?"

"It starts and finishes at a pub."

"Alright, I'll do it."

The advantage of sharing a lift with six or seven other runners in the back of a windowless van was in not being tethered to your own car, which meant post-race drinking and not worrying about getting home. Some of the team were planning to stay the night at the local bunkhouse, The Star, a centre for walkers attempting to climb Pen-y-Fan, while others had brought small tents to pitch up somewhere after dark. Still others were trusting to luck, knowing that the back of Hughie's van (with or without Sheba) was always a last, the very last, the have-to-be-blind-drunk last resort.

Wales held a special attraction for the Pudsey & Bramley team. Two years earlier, after a British Championship counter at the Moelwyn Peaks Race – a 9.5-mile route across several mountain peaks, with over 2600ft of craggy climbing – most of the team ended up, along with a handful of Bingley Harriers, in the nearest pub where some of the locals didn't take too kindly to the Yorkshire team's exuberant post-race party. Over-exuberant, some might say. Provocatively over-exuberant, perhaps. Possibly provocative, loud, annoying, outrageous and over-exuberant. The outcome was that the locals decided to take back their right to be more provocative and annoying than the incomers and began to hurl insults. Insults that, frankly, stated their territorial rights in the manner that Welsh folk have had to do for centuries against their overbearing English neighbours. There were beer glasses chucked and punches thrown and epithets hurled, all of which culminated in the arrival of the gallant Welsh Police Force, or *Heddlu Gogledd Cymru,* as they are known locally. The Heddlu arrived in a tatty squad car that screeched to a halt in much the same way as police cars used to do on *Z-Cars*, thus alerting the scrappers to their presence. Runners and locals fled the pub, dodging the two Heddlus before sprinting off in every direction. Gary Devine was, of course,

among those heading off swiftly down the main street, sprinting into a garden and clearing a fence and hedge before the chasing bobby gave up.

In the earlier afternoon's fell race, under a cloudless sky and with tinder-dry conditions underfoot, Gary had finished fourth, holding off the legendary Billy Bland on a fast descent. The late evening's drunken road race, under a moonlit sky and with a trail of spilt beer underfoot, led to the capture, by the constabulary, of Pudsey & Bramley's Paul Stevenson. A dependable and long-standing member of the club, Paul was a brilliant all-round runner whose only handicap was an inability to move fast after a handful of pints of Welsh bitter. At the best of times, Paul ran with a definite lean to the left, possibly the result of unequal leg-lengths – but as a fiercely loyal P&B athlete he'd been a top competitor on the road, on cross-country and on the fells, leaning or not. As the rest of the team sprinted off into the village shadows with the locals hurling insults after them, Paul was rugby tackled by several newly-arrived back-up police officers and bundled into the back of the car as much to protect him from the Welsh lynch mob as anything else, taking him to the station and charging him with affray. He was released several hours later, partially sober and desperately angry at being abandoned by the rest of his team-mates, and bailed to appear at the local magistrates' court in several weeks' time.

Throughout all the commotion, Gary's dad Hughie had remained seated in the corner of the pub, occupying an ornate wooden bench seat and refusing to leave a half-empty pint behind. It was Hughie who'd driven the team down that morning in his builder's van while everyone played a four-hour marathon of *Trivial Pursuit* in the back, seated on scattered kitbags around the ubiquitous upturned wheelbarrow.

Orange question, sport and leisure –
Which former British Fell Running champion also represented
England in the 3000m steeplechase at the 1978 Commonwealth

Games in Calgary?
(Answer below)

By dint of having arrived at the pub well over an hour before the Pudsey & Bramley team (they were busy running up and down the Moelwyn Peaks), Hughie had befriended the locals to the point where the landlord was enjoying his tales of having played rugby league to a high standard, even joining him in occasional whisky toasts to famous Welsh rugby players. Later, as the insults had started to fly, Hughie quietly supped his drink and watched as the rumpus erupted. When the police, with Paul Stevenson safely locked in the back of their car, came in to investigate how the fracas had started, Hughie simply told them that the provocative, loud, annoying and outrageous English team were called Clayton Harriers and were from Lancashire. This might have done the trick had Hughie not then decided to totter unsteadily out of the pub and attempt to get into his van to drive off – where, despite being unable to get his key into the ignition, he was arrested for being drunk in charge of a vehicle.

That was all ancient history now, albeit a history that left Stevie with a permanent grudge. While the Pen-y-Fan Championship race didn't boast the long, tough distance of either the Moelwyn Peaks or the British Army's 'Fan Dance' route (and nor did the runners have to carry a heavy pack), it did have one of the fastest, steepest descents in the entire mountain racing calendar. Shortly after the summit is reached along a stony track that winds up along the skyline ridge, the race drops off northwards down a grassy slope that descends, from the summit to the finish, 580 vertical metres in 2,450 metres horizontally. This particular descent is seen as the perfect gradient for super-fast running; any steeper would mean having to continually 'brake' in order to avoid toppling forward and rolling, stone-like, to the bottom. Other descents – in particular, off Scafell Pike – have a similarly steep gradient but are far too rough underfoot to avoid braking.

On the starting line at Pen-y-Fan were an assortment of elite runners who, typically for British fell racing, came in all shapes and sizes. Look at any top-class athletic event – 100m sprint or 5k race, for instance – and you'll see that in each branch of the sport there's a general body-type, an optimum frame size. Of course there are exceptions, but the events themselves tend to determine the body shapes of its top competitors. The start line at Pen-y-Fan was a reminder that fell runners, having to contend with wildly different disciplines, often within a single race, don't tend toward the same physique and build. Shaun Livesey, Rossendale AC, short and nimble. Keith Anderson, Ambleside AC, tall and lean. Andrew 'Scoffer' Schofield, Rochdale AC, heavy and broad-shouldered. Colin Donnelly, average height but powerful build. All these runners excelled at different aspects of the sport, each favoured different conditions underfoot, different weather, short or long courses, rocky or grassy, stormy or sunny. Some were brilliant and natural navigators, others were prone to getting lost and ending up at the foot of the wrong valley. Some loved tumbling down loose Lakeland scree, leaping and crashing down the moving, slipping surface. Some loved the bitter cold, stomping through fresh snow-drifts. Some preferred the so-called *Long A's*, the races categorised as over 20 kilometres in distance (often much more) and averaging not less than 50 metres of climb per kilometre (often much more). A *Long A* also had to have less than 20% of the race distance on road (often much less). These were generally mountain horseshoe routes that took in several high peaks, along with scrambles and route-finding. Some preferred the *Short C's*, fast blasts of less than 10 kilometres with not much climbing or descending.

Short, medium, long. Different horses for different courses, different weathers, different terrain. All the top runners knew the differing strengths of their opponents, and each would look at a race route knowing where the others would be catching or catchable. The ascent of Pen-y-Fan – a steep, steady grind – favoured Colin Donnelly,

Andy Peace, Shaun Livesey, and in the women's race Edinburgh's damn-near-invincible Tricia Calder. Tough, relentless and brilliant climbers the lot of them. But everyone there – all those vying for the top handful of places, those racing for Championship points – knew that when they turned at the summit, it would be Keith Anderson's type of descent; extremely fast, and not rough enough to slow him down. The weather would play a part in the race, too. Gary favoured cold, wet, windy weather, anything unsettling and off-putting. He liked it when other runners complained of the icy conditions, when they wore gloves and long sleeves and tights and hats and even balaclavas, as if to say, this is going to be hard, I don't like this, I'm worried, almost as if they were already making excuses. Gary was happiest looking unconcerned and unruffled, a tatty vest, battered shoes and a grin, and if it was bucketing it down then all the better. Punk, innit?

Punk's undignified entry into the heart of British culture in the late 1970s brought with it a change of pace and style. The teens at St Mary's who were into their music, lads mainly, who wore the badges and went to concerts, who hogged the sixth-form common room record player at lunchtime, who wore aviator spectacles and tried desperately to grow their hair long, were listening to Genesis and Mike Oldfield, Pink Floyd and Yes. Those were the gateway drug to the schoolboy horrors of prog rock, deeper and deeper into what the punks would see as the abyss that was Rick Wakeman, ELP and Rush. And further: Tangerine Dream, Caravan, Barclay James Harvest, Jethro Tull. Album tracks sometimes took up whole sides of vinyl, with meandering keyboard solos and titles labelled as 'suites' and 'movements'. This was music to gently nod your head to, music to do your maths homework to. Bands didn't release singles, singles were for teenyboppers – this was music to take seriously. Calculated, polished, impeccably played. Those that didn't want to follow the longhairs down the rabbit hole made do with ELO, The Eagles, Queen and Bryan Ferry, all with similarly immaculate production, note-perfect and flawlessly smooth.

Punk was different, it was defiantly about singles, the shorter the better, rough and ready, wham-bam-thank-you-ma'am. The first punk record was The Damned's 'New Rose' clocking in at just over two-and-a-half minutes, a scorched earth blast of noise. "I can't stop to mess around," sang Dave Vanian, setting the pace for every other punk band to follow. It wasn't just about speed and length, it was about urgency, getting the song written, recorded, pressed and in the shops as fast as possible. Can't stop, we've got things to say. Joey Ramone, lead singer of New York punks the Ramones, declared, "Play before you get good, because by the time you get good, you're too old to play." It was music with the rough edges left on, music that didn't need 48-track mastering and a catering budget, music that was of the moment, instant, on-the-spot and up-to-date and don't look back and whatever you do, don't make long-term plans because there's NO FUTURE.

Even as the Championship season unfolded, Gary had little thought for the future. He could manage two, three weeks in advance, and would throw in a rough idea of what his summer might look like – essentially, heading off to the continent to compete in whatever uphill-only mountain races would pay for his accommodation – but planning a season around just six competitive Championship races was a leap too far. It wasn't an attitude that punk taught him; it was an attitude that, as he'd discovered back in 1981 when he first gazed at that Dead Kennedys album sleeve, he'd had all along. He'd carried the attitude through school, through home, through his running; only now he had a name for it.

By the time the Pen-y-Fan race came along – three months and two races into the Championship season – and by the time the leading contenders were lining up at the start, it was clear who might be contesting the year's races. There were mostly focussed athletes, fit and ready, their seasons prepped and planned. Obviously things could go wrong – sustaining such a high level of fitness throughout the fell running season was bound to risk injury and fatigue. But essentially, here were a dozen or more runners who were aiming for a top spot as British Fell Running Champion. Further down the field there were those aiming to do well in the different age categories, those just wanting to complete the season's Championship races, those there for the team points; but all eyes were on that bunch of elite runners flung together from all over Britain who saw the warped table-top summit of Pen-y-Fan as another essential step towards Championship points and the eventual title.

Gary, it went without saying, didn't quite fit in. He took his running, and his racing, seriously; he would love to have a crack at the British Championship – as last year's English Championship winner, he knew that he was in with a chance. But he knew that meant being single-minded, even fixated. It meant planning and preparing, it meant looking forward and scheduling, having a timetable and an itinerary. Even the thought of the word 'schedule' made him involuntarily switch off and disengage. Planning a season's races was, simply, not something he was able to do – it was hard enough navigating each week, fitting in gigs, parties and work in with the twice-daily training runs. In the two weeks after this race, Gary's muddled schedule would include trips to Leeds's Duchess of York venue to see D.O.A. (seminal Canadian hardcore punk), Corrosion of Conformity (American punk thrash) and GBH (studs, bristles and brutal guitar noise) along with fitting in the classic Yorkshire Three Peaks race held before the end of April.

Gary liked his running to fit with his music, rough 'n' ready, of the moment. Of course he wanted to run the Championship races, but if something else came up, then … and there was the problem of over-racing, too. Gary wasn't alone in this; despite the Championship format being changed from a compulsory best-six-results-from-nine-races to a more easily achievable best-four-from-six, several of the top runners just couldn't stop themselves running in their favourite and local races. Perceived wisdom (or rather, tried and tested wisdom) among athletes said that rest, repair and quality training sessions should replace races that weren't essential, but nonetheless a lot of fell runners ran not just to compete but to enjoy the fells, to get out on the hills and mountains, to meet friends and team-mates, to climb up and see the world. Gary never kept a race diary, never logged his training, never had a coach and found it difficult to see beyond the next race. Fell racing was something that defined him, defined the way he ran through life: it was in the moment, a joy, an escape, and it was punk.

Something's happening and it's happening right now
You're too blind to see it
Something's happening and it's happening right now
Ain't got time to wait
I said something better change!
　　　— (The Stranglers, 'Something Better Change')

Today wasn't Gary's kind of weather – it was sunny, warm even, clear and dry. Up at the front, the pre-race chat, filtering through the start-line's nervous laughter and mickey-taking, was about the descent, about the severity of the slope and about the number of top names who'd travelled all the way here to race; a who's who of British fell running.

"What d'you reckon then. You fit?"

This was the deep Lancashire burr of Andy 'Scoffer' Schofield, a young 6'3" lad from deepest, darkest Rochdale who had a reputation for winding people up. He wore the black vest of his home town club, pock-marked with white paint flecks; Scoffer was a painter and decorator and every item of clothing he owned was spattered with Dulux household off-white matt. He always got on with Gary, liked to have a laugh with him. He knew he'd never get a straight answer out of him, knew that Gary would never give anything away.

"Fit enough to beat you," replied Gary. It came with a wink and enough of a grin to make it the right side of arrogant. Scoffer laughed.

"It's not me you need to be beating."

Gary understood what Scoffer meant – a quick glance around and he could see Colin Donnelly doing slow and careful stretches, England international Andy Peace chatting to up-and-coming fell star (and nephew of Billy) Gavin Bland, while up the track was Mark Prady (himself a brilliant descender) muttering quietly to Mark Rigby; over there by the wall were two out-and-out climbers, Graham Schofield and Shaun Livesey, and Dark Peak long-distance specialist Andy Trigg, tall and serious, alone in his own thoughts, wearing what the Pudsey & Bramley runners referred to as the Dark Peak club's 'shit-brown' vest.

Scoffer didn't give up.

"I've heard there's a piece of Welsh slate for the winner."

"Mi' dad'd appreciate that, he's doing some roofing in Leeds next week."

"I didn't know they had roofs in Leeds."

Gary smiled. "Ha. I just wish they'd get us going."

"Why, you got somewhere to go?"

"Yeah. The pub. I'll be in there by the time you finish."

"Great, mine's a pint."

Gary knew, as did the rest of the elite runners, that the way to win – or at least, the way to do well – was to build up a gap on the ascent between himself and Keith Anderson that was simply too big for the notorious descender to close.

"How far d'you think you have to have on Keith at the top then?"

"Half an hour."

"The record's about 35 minutes."

"Yeah, like I say, half an hour."

A whistle blew to bring the runners to a semblance of order.

Shuffle, mutter, laugh, look down, look up, quiet, shhh, wait for it –

And they were off. Straight from the whistle, 200 metres up the old cart track, the 1, 2, 3 was Donnelly, Peace, Devine. Not a firm of crooked lawyers but the current fell racing podium placings, Britain's finest and fastest. They began the grassy climb towards the summit ridge, steadily stringing out the 120-odd runners, a line of uneasy puffing and panting that stuttered, broke and stretched as they all climbed the stile and kept to the right side of the valley, still climbing, still the same 1, 2, 3. Keith Anderson was back in sixth or seventh place, wheezing uncomfortably but crucially hanging on, thirty seconds behind the leaders. Donnelly and Peace – weren't they a 1970s moustachioed cop duo? – began to move away from Gary, who was caught by Clayton's Graham Huddlestone as the crocodile followed the mountain's main ridge and passed a large stone obelisk.

This was a monument to the memory of Tommy Jones, a five-year-old boy who got lost and died there in 1900. Jones had been out walking with his cousin William and when the two became separated the little boy, disorientated, disappeared. The search for the boy went on for almost a month, until his body was found high on the mountain's ridge. The boy still wore around his neck his favourite toy tin whistle. From this point on the route to the peak of Pen-y-Fan the runners had been warned about the sweeping drop to the left of the path, a dramatic precipice with a view right across the valley. The stone obelisk didn't so much act as a remembrance for little Tommy but as a reminder to watch out, to be careful.

From here the runners started up the steepest part of the climb, on to the top of Corn Du and on, on, on to the large, open summit of Pen-y-Fan. At the summit, Andy Peace and Colin Donnelly were still neck-and-neck, some 15 seconds ahead of Gary and Graham Huddlestone. A further 20 seconds behind was Keith Anderson, on his own, lifting his head to see the quartet in front of him dropping off the ridge and heading at breakneck pace down the mountain, northwards back to the finish. The front four began to stretch and gap each other, hurtling down the incredibly steep grassy descent, maintaining their positions as they crossed several small gullies. Colin Donnelly's descent time, from summit to finish, was not far under eight minutes – fantastically quick. Andy Peace finished 30 seconds later, Gary a further ten seconds behind Andy.

That's not the end of the story, though.

Keith Anderson's descent that day has gone down in the history books as the fastest sustained descent rate ever recorded in any mountain race. He overhauled a deficit of over a minute and a half to complete his descent in just seven minutes, beating the surprised Colin Donnelly – himself a noted descender – by just two seconds at the finish. In just a few years Anderson had gone from being a (literal) also-ran to a race winner, using his thorough knowledge of science and technology to monitor, test and adjust his training patterns. His running schedules were built on heart rate monitoring and regular testing of blood lactate levels, running many of his speed sessions on a treadmill in order to be able to complete them in a controlled environment. The juxtaposition of the meticulously-prepared Keith against the mountain specialist Donnelly and the seemingly unflappable and inscrutable Devine was a great set-up for the Championship, Keith's win meaning he was right back in the mix for the overall victory. Bring it on. Other notable contenders were Shaun Livesey in 8th, Gavin Bland in 10th and Mark Rigby in 12th. All three could look forward to improving results as the season progressed as they were known to be better at the longer distance races, the boggy slogs and the craggy peaks.

The Pudsey & Bramley team – suitably dazed and disorientated from another four-hour journey in the builder's van, followed by a sub-one-hour dash up and down South Wales' highest peak, were first to the pub. There they stayed most of the evening, an odd one or two disappearing back up north to compete in the following morning's Yorkshire Three Peaks race. An evening in a Welsh pub – what could possibly go wrong? At one point, club member Alan Greenwood, in conversation with local Saturday-night drinkers, pulled down his trousers to reveal a pair of Union Jack underpants, under the mistaken impression that this might be an insult, forgetting that Wales was also part of the Union. Everybody laughed.

(Answer to Trivial Pursuit question: John Wild, British Fell Racing Champion 1981 and 1982.)

CHAPTER 4

"To put it mildly, I was not into sports. I found out quickly that I was the worst athlete in school."
— Jello Biafra, Dead Kennedys

Hughie Devine got up, folded his newspaper, threw it onto the couch, and shouted up the stairs of the large Yorkshire-stone family house that stood guard beside the A65, five minutes' run from the foot of Ilkley Moor:

"Are you coming or what?"

Music rang and boomed from 15-year-old Gary's bedroom. Loud, relentless, searing, ferocious, unyielding music. Music to shake the furniture and rattle the windows. Music to frighten the dogs. Music to make your parents shout 'Turn it down!' from the floor below.

"Gareeeeeeee!"

The music stopped.

"Yeah?"

"Are you coming? We need to get off if you want a proper run."

Every Saturday, Hugh bundled his two sons into his builder's van – a white Transit with the back seats removed and replaced with an upturned wheelbarrow covered by a piece of carpet – and drove them out to his sister's house near the tiny village of Airton in the Yorkshire Dales. Gary's sisters Lynne (older) and Maureen (younger) never came along, why would they? Airton was boring, there was nothing there except a little river and a post office and a tea shop and a farm shop and a Quaker Meeting House and a surrounding landscape of hill after hill after hill, and Auntie Maureen's house was cramped and cold unless you were in the kitchen with its big Aga stove; but as Lynne would tell you, the television wasn't in the kitchen, it was in the living room where Uncle Gordon sat watching his wrestling on Saturday afternoons, ITV's *World of Sport* big bouts, Jackie Pallo, Giant Haystacks, Big Daddy, Kendo Nagasaki, Mick McManus and Les Kellett and what teenage girl wants to spend her Saturday afternoons watching wrestling on a black-and-white television?

From Auntie Maureen's house Gary could head off for a two-hour run up and down the limestone hills that rolled out northwards, Haw Crag and Bell Busk and on to Malham and Gordale, while his younger brother Bradley worked his way through a huge bag of crisps, fixated on the wrestling. Gary was training on his own now that his dad couldn't keep up, his unplanned and untutored running schedule mixing with the twice-a-week planned-and-tutored training sessions over at Bingley Harriers. Running with the Bingley athletes was a definite step up for Gary, not least because it offered him some real competition – on Tuesday night track sessions, he had to make an effort to keep up with lads like Andy Peace, Steve Brooks and Stevie Green, all cherry-picked from the local area as outstanding athletes and all competing nationally as Juniors.

The Bingley Harriers set-up wasn't like it was at St Mary's, it was proper, punishing track work, learning about aerobic and anaerobic power, heat adaptation and dehydration, perception of distance, injuries, paarlauf and fartlek sessions, stuff that Gary had little interest in. It wasn't that he didn't understand the importance of all this attention to detail … just that it somehow didn't fit with his haphazard and spontaneous approach to life. A track session would mean warm-ups and warm-downs, interval sprint repeats, relays with minimum recovery periods, timed circuits and hill reps. It was a world away from the steady moorland running Gary had been used to, and it sharpened and honed his natural ability – and seeing his improvement,

Terry Lonergan was keener than ever to encourage Gary's raw talent, hoping he might switch from cross-country and fells onto the more disciplined and focussed track events, in particular the 3000 metres steeplechase.

Gary had other ideas. He'd been hearing about another band from California called MDC – Millions of Dead Cops – and was desperate to buy their first eponymous album, a 14-track so-fast-it's-blurred onslaught of American hardcore punk. Gary hadn't heard the band, but he knew they were being mentored by Dead Kennedys and he'd heard the song titles and that was enough.

'America's So Straight'
'Born to Die'
'Corporate Deathburger'
'John Wayne Was a Nazi'
'Dick for Brains'
'I Hate Work'
etc, etc, etc.

The problem was, he was completely skint. Down to his last 50p skint. He'd spent £8 on a studded leather belt and some peroxide hair bleach and didn't have any money – he could never get a Saturday job like the other kids because that was when he did his long runs, and he'd long since given up his evening paper round when it started to get in the way of training. He walked across the landing to Bradley's bedroom to ask if he could borrow some money. Bradley asked him what it was for, snorted with laughter when Gary told him, and then said no, he had no money anyway.

The solution might lie in the afternoon's trip to Airton to Auntie Maureen's house. An hour or so in the van with his dad might be enough time to convince him to give him a lift up to Ambleside the following week to take part in the annual professional fell race that climbed up from Rydal Park up to Sweden Crag, around 800 feet of climb in less than a mile. Even in the Juniors race, the prize money – which came in sealed brown envelopes at the finish line, dished out by friendly, ruddy-faced old-timers – would be between £5 and £25 depending on his position. Proper money. Gary thought the courses were too short but the money made it worth the drive.

Gary appeared at the top of the stairs, ready to go and with his kitbag swung over one shoulder. Hugh glanced up, froze for a second, and exploded.

"What the bloody hell's that!?"

Gary slowed as he descended the steps.

"What's what?"

"You bloody know what. What've you done to your hair? You look like a bloody ponce! I hope that washes out!"

"It's bleached. You can't wash it out."

"And who's been at it with the garden shears?"

"I cut it myself."

"You can't turn up at your auntie's with that. You'll give her a heart attack. Get a bloody hat on or we're not going anywhere."

The whole journey there was spent in silence, Bradley in the back fidgeting on the uncomfortable wheelbarrow and Gary wearing a black woollen hat pulled low. He kept it on as they arrived at his auntie's house, lacing up his tatty studded running shoes on the smooth stone flags outside the back door. His uncle Gordon was round the side of the house drawing deeply on a sneaky cigarette – chest problems and a partially-collapsed lung weren't going to stop him dragging on his Players No 6 no matter how much Maureen waved her finger and nagged. Gordon had one leg, and his false limb never seemed to be the right length, giving him an awkward and lop-sided look. Gary wandered around the side of the house, knowing that Gordon was always quick with a sly wink and, with a bit of luck, a five-pound note.

"A'right Gordon."

"Gary."

"Not looking good for United, is it?"

"You're bloody telling me, lad. Never been right since Revie left."

"Think they'll go down?"

"I bloody do. Five or six on the bounce isn't it now? Can't buy a win. That Frank Worthington looks alright though. You never know."

"Fifty grand, he'd better be alright. He'll be collecting his pension at the end of the season."

"Hey, watch it. Nowt wrong wi' getting old."

Gordon winked, as Gary knew he would. Fished around in his pocket. Gary could hear the change but was hoping for a note.

"Here you go. Don't tell your dad. And if you get some sweets, share 'em wi' Bradley."

"I will. Thanks, Gordon."

Five pounds. A fortune worth its weight in supercharged Californian hardcore punk.

Gary waved a quick ta-ra and set off trotting along the stony lane that led out of the village and up onto the open fells. As soon as he was out of sight, the hat came off. He pushed and shoved at his flattened hair until it stuck out at angles. As he rounded the corner and crossed the stone bridge over the River Aire he could see the skyline of Malham Cove up ahead, a majestic white limestone wall that rose up from the earth. He headed for it, looked at his watch, felt the first few drops of rain and smiled.

*

A long, rainy and very loud month later, Gary was at home with his headphones on, sitting on his bed and staring blankly at a school exercise book. It was Hughie that had convinced him to stay on at school to take A levels, pushing him to choose economics, geography and maths statistics, subjects that would mean he could get a good job in the building industry but not have to work outside. Gary had no interest in economics, geography and maths statistics, and little enthusiasm for a job in the building industry. He'd been doing weekend stints as an apprentice with his dad's firm, but what that really meant was an occasional Saturday carrying bricks, fixing up scaffolding and mixing mortar. It was usually outdoors and, apart from the lifting and carrying, pretty easy work. School, on the other hand –

He looked at the sheet of paper in front of him and looked and looked and looked and looked until the print began to blur first into a light fuzz and then slowly into a sprawled, blotchy nothingness.

Answer all questions.

- Use black ink or black ball-point pen. Pencil should only be used for drawing.

- Do all rough work in this answer book. Cross through any work that you do not want to be marked.

- The maximum mark for this paper is 80.

- The marks for questions are shown in brackets.

- No deductions will be made for wrong answers.

Which one of the following applies to merit goods?

A   Their marginal private benefit is greater than their marginal social benefit.

B   They are likely to be provided by the market.

C   They can only be supplied by the
    government.

D   They have the characteristics of non-
    excludability and non-rivalry.

After a month of arguments and accusations, Gary had been ordered to wear the house headphones when listening to his music. This suited him fine; it locked him into a completely separate universe, a head-sized world of confrontational rock 'n' roll racket, and it meant that nobody could tell if he was doing his homework or mouthing along to MDC's 'Born to Die':

I'm born to die
I'm born to fry
My life in a cage
Show my outrage
I'm misunderstood
I did what I could
I made my try
I was born to die

Gary liked working for his dad, even as a kid, liked the outdoors and the physicality of it. He had a knack for the trade, and Hughie could see it – it wasn't just about wheeling a barrow or learning plumbing joints, it was initiative and planning, resourcefulness when things went wrong, gumption. Gary had gumption in spades, the only thing he didn't enjoy about it was being told what to do. Yes Dad, no Dad, where do you want this Dad? Worse than that was the idea of spending another few years studying merit goods and marginal benefits and the characteristics of non-excludability just so he could be told what to do by someone else, indoors. He was beginning to realise that being told what to do was the same whether it was indoors or outdoors. A long, slow death. Born to die. Born to fry. Life in a cage. Show my outrage.

Gary's bedroom door opened and his mum popped her head around. She said something which he couldn't hear, mouthing words like she was a fish in a bowl, waving an arm to motion for him to take off his headphones. He pulled them off his head and burst into a world he'd been a million miles from.

"– at the door."

"Eh?"

"A chap at the door."

"What?"

"A MAN. AT THE DOOR. For you."

"Oh."

He put the headphones on the cabinet next to the bed and swung his legs down on the floor, stretching. He picked up the economics worksheet and tossed it purposely off the other side of the bed.

"What's he want?"

Gary's mum looked impatient and rolled her eyes.

"How do I know what he wants? He's talking to your dad. From Bingley Harriers."

At the door, Gary's dad was small-talking to an older bloke with over-sized glasses and a comb-over. Hughie clearly hadn't invited the man inside, which puzzled Gary. If he was from Bingley Harriers, why was Dad keeping him standing on the front doorstep?

"Gary, this is Arthur."

"Hello, Gary," said Arthur, smiling a smile that gave nothing away. Absolutely nothing.

"Right."

"Tell him what you're here for," said Hughie, and there was something in the way he said it, something with a bit of an edge. Not nasty, just … *a bit sideways*, as Auntie Maureen used to say.

"Well what it is Gary, we've had, a sort of, had a letter, an official letter, um, sent to the club, sent to the Harriers, and as part of the Northern Counties Association, we're duty-bound to pass on the, um, pass on the –"

He was decidedly fidgety, and at this point Gary realised he was holding a letter, an open sheet that he was gripping tightly. Judging by his shuffling and stammering and the way he was glancing up at Hughie, it was clear that Arthur had already revealed the contents of the letter to Hughie and that it hadn't been warmly received.

"– well, pass on the warning."

Warning? All he did at Bingley training nights was warm up and run and sweat and puff and pant and warm down, how could he be given a warning? Was it his hair? Was his kit too scruffy? His running spikes too blunt? His vest un-ironed? His smirk too cocky, too uppity?

"What it is Gary, is that, well, shall I read what they've said? That might be, might be the best way –"

Poor Arthur held the letter up and scanned it, looking for the relevant part to read. Hughie was silently enjoying Arthur's discomfort – go on then, he was thinking, go on and read it again. Fidget and shuffle for all you're worth, Arthur, but I'm not helping you on this, you can bloody well read it all out again. To the teenage lad here, the baffled teenage lad who hasn't a clue what you're on about.

"The Northern Counties blah blah Amateur Athletics Association statutes and rules, which in part, blah blah, um, here's the part – restricting participation in professional sports and not adhering to the amateur code, the junior athlete Gary Devine was a prize-winner at the Ambleside Open Fell Race, a competition held outside the amateur rulings, and won a cash prize at said race. This is in direct contravention of the Three A's statutes and we can only advise you to warn Devine clearly and on the record about both his participation in the race and his, um, yes, his accepting of a cash prize. Please respond, informing us that said athlete understands and accepts our position and please pass on the warning that if Devine takes part in any further professional or non-amateur athletics meetings we will have no choice but to implement a ban on taking part in amateur events. Yours, blah blah, um, that's about the long and short of it –"

Arthur folded the letter and pushed it into his pocket. He looked at Gary, Gary looked at Arthur. Gary felt cornered, quietened. He knew other lads who were running both amateur and professional codes, knew the organisers at both sets of races, couldn't work out why finishing in the top handful of places at Ambleside Sports would cause a chain of events culminating in someone sitting down at a typewriter to tap out an official letter of complaint.

"I know it's a lot of, um, stuff and nonsense, but, rules are rules Gary, and the Northern Counties has to answer to the national Association. That's why they – that's why they, um, anyway. There you have it."

"Right then," nodded Hughie, pointedly. Meaning, the conversation's over then, maybe you ought to be on your way.

"Indeed. Yes. Well, thank you for your time. Hope to see you down at the club, Gary. Keep up the good work."

Arthur whatsisname about-turned and walked crisply back to his car, a burnt orange Montego. The door shut behind him.

Inside, Gary looked at his dad and his dad looked at Gary and then Gary's mum came out into the hallway and looked at the pair of them, standing there. Hughie broke the silence.

"How about this for an idea. You stop doing the professional races, get shut of this malarkey, blokes coming round to the house with their Montegos and official warnings and whatnot. Stop doing the open races, but if you come top three in the amateur races, I'll put a couple of notes in a little envelope for you. How's that?"

With that, Hughie ruffled the top of Gary's hair and the world began to right itself.

CHAPTER 5

"O for a life of Sensations rather than of Thoughts!"
— *John Keats*

High Royds Hospital in Menston was an ominously Gothic psychiatric facility tucked away behind high stone walls off the main A65 road that ribboned along the Wharfe valley. The main belfry housed a single bell which marked the hours, day and night, and local rumour had it that in the building's dark past, every time the bell tolled, an inmate was hanged at the hospital's pumping station. Gary's cousin (or second cousin, to be exact) Jan had ended up in High Royds after handing himself in at a police station while high on shoplifted Evo-Stik. Not just once, but again and again and again and again and again and again, enough times to temporarily turn his brain into mashed potato. After spending a few weeks in the hospital impressing the psychiatrist enough to avoid having electric shock treatment, Jan was granted weekend leave. His first port of call – not least since it was just around the corner – was Gary's house, where he knew he'd be welcomed and looked after in among the weekly family gatherings with Sunday roasts and dogs and a big garden and kids running up and down the stairs and Hughie entertaining everyone and cracking the lids off bottles of ale.

Gary sat on his bed listening to something LOUD, it was a Sunday lunchtime and he was shutting out the babble and guffaw of adults gathered in the living room directly below his room. Jan knocked on the door then came in, pulled along by the music.

"Oh. Jan. I thought they'd locked you up."

"They did. I started a riot and everyone escaped."

"Oh."

"I didn't really. I promised to be good. And your dad had to sign something to vouch for me. So what's this you're listening to?"

"Mass of Black. It's a demo tape. A lad at school knows 'em. Good innit?"

"Never heard of 'em. I should get you a cassette of my band."

"You're in a band?"

"Yeah. Playing guitar."

Gary was impressed. His actual cousin, playing actual guitar in an actual band.

"What are you called?"

"We were called Virus a couple of months ago. But we thought that was a bit short so we changed it to Virus Vengeful and The Evil Dog-Men. Then we thought that was too long so we changed it to The Plague, but we saw there was another band called The Plague. So we haven't got a name right now."

"Who's in the band?"

"Nobody you know. Stu and Tom, Cookridge punks. They came round our house 'cos they knew I played guitar, but when they came round I had my hand all bandaged up from an accident when I was sniffing glue. So I told them I couldn't play anything to show them, but they said they didn't care, so I joined 'em anyway. So now we just need a name. And a bass player."

The music came to an end abruptly, when the cassette ran out halfway through a song. The silence filled up the space more than the music had done. Gary knew that Jan had been in High Royds because his mum worked there as a nurse, but he didn't feel like asking anything more about it. Jan knew that Gary knew but didn't feel like talking about it.

Jan broke the silence first.

"Are you still listening to Hazel O'Connor?"

"No. Our Bradley's got that LP now. I'm into Dead Kennedys now. And The Damned, and Peter & The Test Tube Babies, and Discharge. But Dead Kennedys mainly."

"Have you heard about that Christmas on Earth Festival?"

"Eh?"

"Christmas on Earth. A punk festival at the Queen's Hall in Leeds. The Damned are playing. It's in December. Anti-Nowhere League, UK Subs and Damned. And about ten other bands. It's all day, five quid on the door. You should come."

"I don't know. Will it be all fights and gobbing and all that?"

"Nah, it'll be great. There's some American bands playing. Have you heard of Black Flag?"

"No."

"They're a bit like Dead Kennedys. Well I mean, they're American."

"When is it?"

"December sometime. I'll find out and let you know."

"Right, yeah."

Gary got up and stretched. Mid-afternoon, time for his long Sunday run. He pulled on some scruffy running shoes that were already laced and tied.

"I'm off up to the moor."

Jan, in tight black denim safety-pinned jeans and hand-painted Doc Marts, his mohair pullover a mess of overstretched holes, looked at Gary's blue-and-purple tights and grimaced.

"I don't know how you've got the nerve to go out wearing them."

*

It was lunchtime at St Mary's, during the daily mad rush of to-ing and fro-ing, noise, school bells and playground yells and screams. Terry

Lonergan stood at the entrance to the school changing rooms with his clutch of runners after a 40-minute slog over heavy, sodden fields, everyone bent double, breathing heavily. He was preparing them for the Yorkshire cross-country trials that weekend. Schools from across the county were competing in a mass race – split between girls' and boys' races, 400 in each – over in Huddersfield. The race would determine who would represent Yorkshire at the English Schools Junior Cross-Country Championships in Sheffield a fortnight later. For a change, Gary had spent the training session towards the back of the group. He didn't feel well. He felt rotten, worse than rotten. His guts felt queasy and he was coughing and spluttering and snotting and sneezing. He thought he might throw up. Terry took him to one side. Gary was the school's best hope for a prestigious Yorkshire vest. Gary was Terry's best hope, too. To Terry, this was everything. One in the eye for the teachers who thought he was mad spending his lunchtimes out in the fields, getting muddied and soaked while they were sucking on Woodbines and necking tea, three sugars, in the staffroom.

"You don't look well Gary."

"I'm not."

"You look like death warmed up."

"I feel like death, sir. Not warmed up."

"Are you going to be alright to race the trials?"

Gary looked puzzled that Terry was even asking. Of course he would run the trials. It wasn't through some dogged, single-minded determination, some will to overcome the odds, to tough it out, fight the flu. He would run the trials because, simply, that's what he did. He ran. It was what he did best, what he enjoyed most, what defined him.

"I'll be right."

Terry looked worried. Then clenched his fist and grinned.

"No pain, no gain, eh?"

Gary had always disliked that slogan. It was a coach's slogan, a Hollywood army sergeant beefing up his recruits slogan, a shoe company marketing slogan. A couple of months earlier, the British film *Chariots of Fire*, with its pumping electronic soundscape overlaying images of plucky, determined, grimacing athletes, had become an international hit. Its tag line, read in one of those deep, gritty, sincere and earnest American voices, declared:

'This is the story of two men who run. Not to run, but to prove something to the world.'

This made no sense to Gary. He ran just to run. He had nothing to prove to the world, and he believed that yes, you *can* have gain without pain – that even his hardest runs could be rewarding and enjoyable, simply because running was the thing that he did, the thing that he loved, the thing that let him feel happiest, fulfilled, fully-realised. The music that played on repeat in Gary's head as he ran, the rhythm he raced to, wasn't a softly pulsing Vangelis synthesiser melody, and it wasn't in soft-focus slow-motion. Today, it was a song by punk-thrash band Discharge, whose album Why? was the new touchstone for heavy, fast, loud, angry punk rock. The song was called 'Ain't No Feeble Bastard' and its raw, repetitive onslaught lasted exactly 90 seconds:

Ain't no feeble bastard
That obeys their every say
They say do this they say do that
No I'm no dogsbody

By the time of the trial race in Huddersfield, Gary was feeling no better. Heavy-legged, sneezy, dull-headed. He knew he had to finish in the top eight to be selected; he also knew that on any other day that would be a cinch, a certainty, all sewn up and locked on. The race began and several hundred schoolboys headed off across the corner of a patchwork of football pitches, heading for sparse woods ranged across a low hillside. Gary stuck with the leaders for a while but his chest was heaving and complaining, he couldn't draw enough breath. Phlegm was rushing to escape and his eyes were stinging and red. The race settled into its pace and behind Gary a long, long line of exhausted runners were making a curving, lengthening tail. Ain't no feeble bastard, ain't no feeble bastard, ain't no feeble bastard, ain't no feeble bastard, through the wheezing and the coughing and the gasping Gary could see that there were seven runners in front of him. He glanced behind, and sensed a gap opening up, knowing that all he needed to do was not allow anyone to pass.

This was how Gary raced. Not to break records, not against the clock, not to prove something to himself (or 'to prove something to the world') but to beat the person behind. This was racing, the simple competitive urge that said 'I can run faster than you'. Gary never wore a watch. It felt like a distraction, it made a run or a race into a series of formulas, it imposed structure, it tried to carve up and explain the beautifully odd, mysterious feeling of running, of winning. Finish in front of the runner behind. That's all you have to do. Eighth. Make the team. Don't die.

He finished eighth. He made the team. He didn't die. He went home and went up to bed, where he slept for 12 hours straight.

The English Schools Junior Cross Country Championships were, for many young runners, the pinnacle of school athletics. Boys and girls who'd proven themselves to be the fastest runner in the school had to prove they were the fastest in the town, then the fastest in the region, then the fastest in the county, before they had a crack at seeing if they could be the fastest in the entire country. Competing at the English Schools also meant being awarded a county vest, something only a handful of runners every year could wear, and getting your picture in the St Mary's school magazine or even the *Wharfedale Observer* or even, even, even the *Yorkshire Post*. It was a big deal, and by the time the race came around Gary had recovered from his bout of flu and jumped aboard the Saturday-morning minibus taking the team down to Sheffield for the national Championship race.

Graves Park in south-west Sheffield was a big, open municipal park that was developed a few years too late to be pock-marked by ornate Edwardian stone features. Instead it became popular as a sprawling green space criss-crossed by streams, woods, football pitches, pitch & putt and an animal farm. The race route plotted a course in and around all the park's attractions, apart from the animal farm, which it kept well clear of, and the football pitches, which were teeming with yelping boys and barking dads at the inter-schools football matches. This being a National Championship race, each county team was herded into narrow holding pens and lined up, one runner behind the other, for the start, in the hope this would prevent a mass pile-up at the gun (and would conveniently 'seed' the runners so that the field could stretch out naturally). This, though, meant that Gary would start at the back of an eight-body line, dictated by his position as last counter in the trials race, knowing that the mad scramble of just under 400 boys being released from the narrow traps one after each other in waves meant that those at the back of the line – all the county's eighth-place counters – were around thirty seconds behind the front-runners as they left their pens.

The course, 4500 metres of muddy grassland and firm woodland trails, wasn't exactly Gary's ideal course, but on the other hand there were several ups and downs, his flu symptoms had gone, he had his Yorkshire vest, and at last he was released from between the taped holding pen to fight his way through the stampede. He felt good, and having to weave and push past slower runners at least gave him a real sense of moving up the field, one by one, boy by boy, place by place. Any race less than 5k felt criminally short, but Gary felt good, and as he moved through the field he was aware of picking off most of the Yorkshire team, one, two, three, four … Hughie and Bradley were there to watch, shouting and screaming as Gary approached the finish, still overtaking, wheezing and wild-eyed but moving fluently and

easily, to cross the line in 9th position overall and second Yorkshire finisher.

Here was confirmation, if he needed it (and he'd say, matter-of-factly, that he didn't) that he was able to race with the best, that his training was paying off, that he could compete against the senior runners, that maybe, just maybe, he could make something of his running. PE teacher Terry Lonergan thought so, coach Gordon Agar thought so, and of course his dad Hughie thought so. In the back of the van on the way home from Sheffield, Hughie wore a proud grin and occasionally slammed the steering wheel as he drove.

"That showed 'em, eh? Bloody showed 'em! I knew you'd do it. Stuffed it right up 'em! Bloody great."

Gary sat on the upturned wheelbarrow, Discharge's thunderous chant rolling round and round in his mind.

Ain't no feeble bastard!
Ain't no feeble bastard!
Ain't no feeble bastard!

CHAPTER 6

"In the women's toilets, a stream of punky blokes were crawling from outside in through the top window, and an assortment of chaps were taking up position around the sinks to perpetuate that curiously individual punk habit of holding court in the Ladies. Meanwhile, a flood was starting at the back of the hall. You had to paddle through it if you felt inclined to go to the bog. It seemed to be coming from the Gents, but I didn't investigate too closely. The party in the women's was continuing."

— Carol Clerk, Melody Maker, reviewing
'Christmas on Earth' Punk Festival, December 1981

Gary was waiting inside the main entrance to Leeds train station, fresh off the Ilkley train, on a cold December morning as Jan walked across the open arrivals hall, grinning. They were both of them excited (but trying not to show it), apprehensive (but trying not to show it) and slightly drunk (and failing not to show it). Between them they'd brought two carrier bags of cans of supermarket cider, surely more than enough to see them through the twelve-hour marathon to come. Gary had already run that morning, an eight-mile easy session from his home in Ilkley up onto the moor, randomly following its maze of paths, tracks and sheep-trods. John – owner of the prized Dead Kennedys album – had managed to get Gary a ticket for what was to be his first proper punk concert, but was making his own way there; so Jan had promised to meet Gary at the train station to help him navigate his way into what seemed to be a curious and impenetrable world where the secret cultural codes were written in a language of spiked hair, leather jackets and fast, loud music.

But nothing, and I mean nothing, prepared Gary for the sight that greeted him as they headed down under the dark railway arches and rounded the corner from Neville Street towards the huge old tram depot that was the Queen's Hall. Hundreds of black-clad fugitives from the planet punk, head-to-toe straps and zips, leather and studs, tartan and spikes, all with their carrier bags of booze and their laughing and their name-calling and their swearing and their shouting, spilling out across the Queen's Hall's front entrance and into Sovereign Street, off the pavement edge, slowing the gawping, tutting, head-shaking general public as it crawled along in the traffic. Gary and Jan surrendered their tickets to the ruffled, hired security blokes blocking the doorway, suits and shiny shoes at Sunday lunchtime, unused to this mad punk parade. Inside the Hall, no seating, no wall hangings, no carpets, nothing but old tram rails left embedded in the floor – tram rails that were iced over with the December cold. An empty black-painted void filled with punks, slouching and sitting and waiting for the noise to begin. And at twelve-thirty precisely, the noise began.

To Gary, even as the first band struck their first power chord, this was confirmation of everything he dared to believe about this messy, unruly sub-culture that'd been worming its way into his head since he'd first heard that Dead Kennedys record. The general air of chaos mixed with camaraderie, name-calling and laughter bled straight into the opening four-chord thrash of London punks Charge, first band of the day, fast and loud and already this all felt special, memorable, important. Jan disappeared into the thickening crowd as punks, hearing the music roaring from the main stage PA, flooded to the front of the hall, shoving and pushing, dancing, itching to move. Gary was swept up in it all, awe-struck and smiling.

Whatever that morning's eight-mile run had taken out of Gary, it didn't compare to the stamina needed to spend an afternoon with umpteen hardcore punk bands, one after each other, crash, smash, crash, ring. As Captain Sensible of The Damned was to say about the day's event, "I've just discovered what this is like! It's like the *Generation Game* – y'know that part at the end when the microwave ovens and the hairdryers go by on the conveyor belt and the contestants have to remember what they've seen. Well, here, they're wheeling the bands on and wheeling them off, and if you ask the punters at the end what groups they saw, they'll never be able to remember them all!"

Later, when anyone would ask Gary about the first gig he went to, he would say, "Christmas on Earth, Queen's Hall. Fourteen punk bands in eleven hours." The noise levels never dipped, from Charge right through to Black Flag, The Exploited, UK Subs and The Damned. Gary's favourites were The Anti-Nowhere League, a bunch of leather-clad bikers from, of all places, Royal Tunbridge Wells. Their cartoonish take on punk was crafted from repeated riffs, obscenities and volume, in any order you fancy.

I've had crabs, I've had lice
I've had the clap and that ain't nice
('So What', Anti-Nowhere League)

When, a decade earlier, David Bowie had declared, "…this ain't rock 'n' roll – this is genocide!" he might have had the Christmas on Earth Festival in mind, Anti-Nowhere League lead singer Animal prowling the front of the stage, bellowing himself hoarse as he loomed above the writhing, burring Hieronymus Bosch of a pogoing, high-kicking, slam-dancing crowd. It was all a glorious mess.

By five o'clock, Gary was drunk and tired but determined not to give up. There were still hours and hours to go and a queue of bands waiting to go on. What he needed to do was sober up, and to sober up didn't mean stop drinking, it meant eating. He pressed into the melee towards the stage, looking for Jan. The general blur of black clothing didn't help. It took several circuits around the hall before he spotted

"Why d'you want to know that?"

"'Cos I'm a veggie. A vegetarian."

"Since when were you a vegetarian?"

"Since a couple of weeks ago. I saw that film at a Crass gig in Todmorden couple of months back. They show a film where animals are, like, in tiny cages and that. All in rows, hundreds of 'em, like factory farming and that. Pigs and chickens. And baby cows and everything. So I thought, right, I'm not eating meat now."

"Oh. Right."

The man behind the counter, dark beard and small paper hat, wiping his hands on his stained apron, looked at Gary.

"You, sir? Yes?"

Gary ummmmmmed and aaaaaahed and weighed up his options. He fancied chicken, or fish, but Jan had put him off with his talk of babies in cages.

"Go on then. I'll have what he's having."

"Just chips?"

"Just chips."

They sat down at a Formica-topped table stained with the small brown pocks of cigarette stubs. Jan was looking through his carrier bag, tallying up how many cans he had left and working out if he could afford to buy a couple more from the newsagent's. Gary was working out whether becoming a vegetarian would affect his running. Would he get tired? Would he lack vitamins and protein? Would he lose muscle bulk? He gave it thirty seconds of thought.

"Is it healthy, being a veggie?"

Jan looked up.

"Yeah. It's better for you. Long as you have Marmite. Vitamin B12."

"Oh. Right."

And by the time they got back to the Queen's Hall, Gary was a vegetarian.

Eight cans down and only the UK Subs and The Damned left to play. This wasn't a gig, it was a marathon. That night Gary learned that if you enjoyed the rough 'n' tumble of the mosh pit, if you needed to let off steam, sober up, feel the physical argy-bargy of a punk crowd, then you threw yourself into the sweaty heart of the dancing and let go of whatever semblance of cool and decorum you left the house with. You stood at the edge watching the whirling melee until, after three, 1, 2, 3, you let yourself fall into its scrapping, flailing centre, and the only way to stay upright was to join the kicking and punching and pulling. After a matter of minutes, which felt like a lifetime of banging and bruising, you heard the song end and the music stop and the crowd roar and you took your chance to move out from the scraggy mess and back to the safety of the crowd. It was a work out. You could mark it down as a training session. It was an all-over, full-body, physical, fast and slow exercising of every muscle and bone and tendon and sinew.

Dancing to UK Subs at Christmas on Earth was where Gary now belonged, where the world didn't just shift on its axis, it toppled and fell. The next morning he would wake up and, like he did every day, drink a glass of water, pull on his knackered running shoes, throw on some running tights and a baggy training top and run for an hour. Morning runs were steady, regular, evenly-paced. Afternoon or evening training sessions, when he had time to do them, were a mixed bag, intentionally varied – fartlek, fast-and-slows, speed work at the track, hill reps up at Otley Chevin. Gary's training was, to all intents and purposes, disciplined and focussed. He was averaging up to 60 miles a week now, and racing every few weeks in the Junior Fell Running Championships. He had his eye on an England vest, on being picked to represent his country in one of the international continental mountain races. And if he was to maintain that notion of sensible level-headedness, that scrupulous, purposeful resolve that came with training – the stuff that takes natural talent and ability and makes it win races – then he needed the balance of dancing to UK Subs playing 'Live in a Car' twice as fast as the recorded version, he needed to see The Damned's drummer Rat Scabies thumping his snare so hard he'd break the skin, crack crack crack crack right into tomorrow morning's headache. It was all in the balance, in the extremes.

Gary didn't want to run along flat, even, straight, predictable pavements, didn't want to run to the perfect tempo-ticking of a stopwatch; but he knew that getting the best out of his running meant having dedication and discipline. He hated those words. Dedication and discipline. But what he found in punk, and specifically in a day of drunken, noisy chaos at the Christmas on Earth Festival, was a way to balance the dedication and discipline with noisy, messy, topsy-turvy disorder.

Sometime before the last band played their last power chord, Gary headed unsteadily outside, turned left under the arches and walked towards the station. Jan had disappeared and the last train to Ilkley had gone, but his sister Lynne and her boyfriend had agreed to pick him up. He climbed into the back seat and tried not to say much as Lynne pointed out punks in various states of disorder wandering up from Queen's Hall.

"Look at the state!"

Lynne's boyfriend edged the car out, changing gear, trying unsuccessfully to keep his eyes on the road.

"Bloody hell. Some right characters out tonight."

As Gary peered out of the window he tried to focus on the day he'd had, but all he could think was that he wanted to rip the knees out of his jeans and he wanted to get his nose pierced and he wanted a leather jacket and he wanted to paint bands on it and he wanted to be part of the enthralling, electrifying and exciting world he'd just discovered.

CHAPTER 7

"It is a myth that homeless people and squatters are one and the same. For a lot of people squatting is a lifestyle. They move from property to property and are often anti-government, making some kind of protest statement. It is those people we have to stop."

— Mike Weatherley, MP

Two bags: one full of clothes and toiletries, one full of running gear. The first one little more than an outsize carrier bag, the second huge, misshapen and overflowing. Gary dumped both on an old mattress positioned untidily in one corner of the room and looked around at his new home, a flat above a strange and secretive shop called *The Sorcerer's Apprentice,* in Burley, Leeds 6. The shop sold all sorts of occult paraphernalia, including strangely-shaped bottles and jars of ready-mixed potions and powders, incense, candles, ornate chains decorated with dragons and crosses, tarot cards, ouija boards and books on all manner of mystic arts. Gary had left school a couple of weeks into the post-Christmas term, without a word of warning, and his dad's ambitions for his son's career as a quantity surveyor disappeared as Gary signed on to the government's Enterprise Allowance Scheme: £40 a week for a year, signing a piece of paper that said you were setting up a business. He wasn't.

The flat had been a rented property until the landlord had somehow (nobody knew how) ended up in prison, whereupon the property became a squat. There were no curtains, but thankfully the window wasn't broken. A bare bulb hanging from a central ceiling rose was the room's only electric light. An old tiled fireplace had a long-unused and rusting gas fire plumbed in front of it, but the fireplace's mantlepiece, heavy ornate stone, had propped on it a beautiful art deco mirror with lined and patterned edging. Apart from the bed and the fire there was very little in the room. "It could do with a clean," was what Gary had been told as he contemplated his new situation.

Leeds 6 was once a fashionable part of the city, just north of the centre and home to a huge and sprawling university campus. Further north was the traditionally Jewish area, and out beyond that were the dense but gardened semi-detached estates up the old Otley Road and on towards the country mansions of Bramhope. It was fifteen miles and a world away from Gary's childhood home in Ilkley, along the Aire valley that carried the river, the railway, the canal and the busy A65 escape route out of Leeds.

But Leeds 6 had changed drastically over several decades of an ever-growing student population, and most of the area's red-brick terraced housing had been converted into flats. For the majority of the houses this 'conversion' meant a hastily-attached lock on the doors of each bedroom, sometimes a sink plumbed awkwardly into the corner of a room, occasionally a framed warning about fire hazards hung beside the front door. There was invariably one shared bathroom and toilet, the bath doubling as a shower with the addition of a stained plastic shower rail and curtain. Grim, grim, grim. Landlords crawled out of a swamp somewhere up near the chemical waste dump along Kirkstall Road and somehow secured loans to buy chains of these terraced houses, each property assessed for damp (tick), wear and tear (tick), dangerous lead pipe plumbing (tick), faulty electrics (tick) and lack of security (tick). Leeds 6 was, throughout the 1980s, the area of the country with the most burglaries per number of properties. Gangs drove over from East Leeds in their crappy old Escorts, Sierras, Astras, Fiestas, Cortinas, Novas, Orions and Metros, waited for students to go to the pub and then filled their cars with 10-speed bikes, hire purchase TVs and portable double-cassette beatboxes.

Nobody cared. Here was a migrating population of students who stayed for a year, two years, three years at most, then disappeared, leaving their rank bedsheets and barely-opened sociology textbooks behind. It was inevitable in this booming scramble for space that the landlords, now able to stand on their hind legs and with hired lawyers, would simply forget about certain properties, or deem them not worth fixing up. Houses would empty out at the end of summer term and just remain deserted, their front doors on a latch and unemptied bins spilling across the pavement. Another inevitability was that someone would eventually spot an untenanted house and pass on its whereabouts to the Leeds Squatters' Estate Agency, a clandestine and largely invisible organisation that existed in and around various shared kitchens across the area from Meanwood to Hyde Park. The LSEA, never having been formally constituted, relied on goodwill, huge pots of soup, gossip, sex, cheap cider, occasional fights, broken tea mugs, sticky carpets, loyalty, pet dogs, fanzines, weekly social security cheques, love, access to a photocopier, hair dye, swearing and loud music, not necessarily in that order. The LSEA hung banners outside empty houses reading things like:

SQUAT NOT ROT!
WHAT IS NOT ALLOWED IS STILL POSSIBLE!
PROPERTY IS THEFT!
WE WILL ASK NOTHING AND DEMAND NOTHING!
OCCUPY!
HOUSING IS A NEED, NOT A PRIVILEGE!
SQUAT THE LOT!

When an empty house was flagged up, a delegation would go round and force an entry, check that no-one was already living there, and padlock the front door. The key to the padlock was then passed on to whoever was first to grab their sleeping bag and get their black-denimed arse around to the property.

*

1981 turned into 1982 against a backdrop of record-breaking sub-zero temperatures and heavy snow and to a soundtrack of Bucks Fizz, ABBA and The Police. It was one of the coldest winters on record, with snow falling continuously in some places for 36 hours. The cross-Pennine M62 motorway was brought to a standstill and trains got stuck in the snow, with passengers being airlifted to safety. Away from the towns and cities, rescue helicopters worked non-stop, taking people to hospital and helping farmers trying to stop their animals from freezing to death. Meanwhile, down in the Meanwood Valley that winds its way northwards out from Leeds 6 and towards the foot of the Yorkshire Dales, Gary stomped and trudged and waded through the drifts to his own soundtrack of loud, rhythmic noise, played and replayed in his head as he kept up his morning training runs, usually arriving back at his flat before the rest of the household stirred.

His sodden running gear was hung to dry on the edge of the bed in front of a two-bar fire, before being stuffed back into the Tardis-like kitbag in the corner. The bag sat there, like Larkin's toad, a symbolic reminder of another life out there on the trails and paths. Apart from the bag and the collection of trophies purposefully *not* on display, there was little to indicate that other life. He had his leather belt, his chopped hair, his small collection of obscure punk cassettes, and blimey, he lived in a squatted house now – but was haunted by the idea that one false move might expose his lack of sufficient punk credentials. There were protocols to observe, etiquette to learn. How many lace holes in your Doc Marts. The circumference of your badges. The width of your trousers. The lack of cleanliness of anything and everything.

He'd been at the squat now for three weeks. He was beginning to get to know the others in the house, but rarely saw them during daylight hours, when he was either on a labouring job with his dad (they were doing out a cellar in Guiseley, turning a damp oversized coal-hole into a fully-plumbed photographic darkroom) or out running. The Sorcerer's Apprentice squatters seemed friendly enough, but due to their differing concept of day and night they'd not yet seen him slipping in and out of the house in Lycra tights and studded running shoes. Not that Gary minded them seeing – he was virtually impossible to embarrass, running tights or not. Water off a duck's back.

One afternoon Gary's mum called round to see him at the flat. She'd come to drop off some clean washing, and to pick up a bin bag of dirty running stuff; she was his mum, and she said *that's what mums do*.

Only this time she wanted to talk.

Gary made them both a cup of tea. Milk in last, they weren't posh. He was puzzled. When they were both sitting at the kitchen table with brews in their hands, she began.

"Me and your dad have split up."

"Right."

"I've moved out. Well, I'm in the middle of moving out."

"Hmm."

"It's been coming for a long time."

"Erm … where are you going?"

"I'm getting a house in Yeadon. This side of the airport. Near the shops. Your dad's threatening to move up to Dacre Banks, he's got work there and I don't suppose he'll be able to afford the Ilkley house for too much longer."

"Right."

"You know what he's like."

"Yeah."

"He's on the whiskey. Your Bradley's staying with him. Maureen's coming with me."

"Right."

"Is that your bag of washing?"

"Yeah."

"Give it here. I'll come round next Thursday and drop it off. Have you anything else needs sorting?"

"No, I'm right."

"Well then. Take care."

"And you."

*

The roots of squatting in Britain go back a long way, right back to 1649 and St George's Hill, where Gerrard Winstanley inspired a group of nonconformists called The Diggers to set up camp on private land and live an egalitarian, shared and self-sufficient life. They were brutally evicted, but their legacy as radical activists was profound. In more recent times, hundreds of soldiers, returning from World War II, only to find themselves homeless, took over empty buildings including disused army barracks and prisoner-of-war camps. They put up net curtains to demonstrate their ownership.

Into the 1970s, and the tail-end of a hippy movement that was growing more militant had become a groundswell of practical, communal living – the new co-operative movement spread across the country and squatting became more popular with the establishment of the Advisory Service for Squatters. It went hand-in-hand with several high-profile and successful attempts at mass squatting, where sometimes whole streets of empty terraces were taken over to house people. It seemed that no matter how hard the authorities clamped down on squatting, they couldn't stop it; it became not just about needing shelter but a way of life, a counter-culture.

Leeds was no exception. During the 1970s there had been various squats set up across the city, and into the 1980s these squats became established. Areas like Woodhouse and Hyde Park were plagued with absentee landlords, who had bought up cheap housing and then left them to rot when their tenants moved out. The squatters got hold of lists of these houses and distributed them, green-lighting a surge in the number of squatted properties in the north Leeds area. In many ways, punk and squatting were made for each other – a simple solution to a complex problem, a do-it-yourself ethos, a scream-and-then-do-it immediacy, and a lack of respect for authority, for cultural norms, for property, for overlords and lawyers, for tradition, for ownership, for 'normal'.

The 1970s sold 'normal' in the shape of Barratt housing estates, semi-detached two-bedroom pink-brick cubes with perfectly-manicured front lawns and neighbours who wouldn't give you your ball back when it went over their fence. Homeowners who tut-tut-tutted at the state of her at number 23, and have you seen what number seven have done to their hedge, and just look at them kids, I swear they haven't seen a bar of soap in a month of Sundays. This was the world of cheap mortgages on new-builds that punk was born into, so it's no surprise that it embraced the squatting movement with such eagerness. The old houses, the discarded buildings, the empty flats – punk came along and moved into them, fixed the electricity, hung curtains, unblocked the loo. And through it all was an openness, a desire to live in a space that wasn't suffocated by family hierarchies – come in, throw a sleeping bag on the sofa, the room's yours mate.

Gary didn't stay at the Sorcerer's Apprentice flat for long; a room came up in a squat in one of the red-brick terraced rows over in Woodhouse, a tightly-packed grid of hundreds of terraced houses that backed onto the Meanwood Valley. The valley, with its wooded and unlit hillsides, had a reputation as a place to get mugged, a place to avoid. The Yorkshire Ripper had murdered and dumped a woman up on one of the valley's steep, rough hillsides. But the valley also offered an escape route from the city out into the countryside. The Meanwood Valley Trail ran practically from the city centre right out to Adel Woods and beyond, to Eccup Reservoir and the southern edge of the Yorkshire Dales. It was perfect for off-road running.

The front ground-floor room that Gary moved into was surprisingly light and even more surprisingly free of damp, a high-ceilinged space with a bay window that looked out onto a small and tatty garden full of bin bags and discarded electrical appliances (a cooker lay on its back with its four short legs sticking out and its door open, as if it had been shot). The house was one of a series of Victorian terraced properties clustered around this small area of Leeds 6, most of them gathering places for long days of smoking hash and long nights of drinking cider.

Bizarrely, the room that became available was a room that Gary's cousin Jan had been living in. Jan had vacated the room temporarily to house-sit at his girlfriend's mum's for a fortnight while she was away on holiday. When Jan returned to his room at the Woodhouse squat he was surprised to find that Gary had moved in.

"Oh. Gary. Er… this is my room."

"What?"

"This is… well, this was my room."

"They said it was empty. Sorry. I've just got settled. Do I have to move?"

"Well, erm… No, you stay. I'll find somewhere."

The anarcho-punk-squatting scene alternated smoking hash and drinking cider with regular gigs in the city centre at venues like Adam & Eve's, The F Club and the Bierkeller. Dark, soulless cellars with too-loud PAs and cheap beer, sticky floors and broken chairs. Places that felt, to Gary, like home. For all the perceived menace of the punk look – the aggressive stencilled lettering on biker jackets, the soaped spiked hair, the boots, the general air of 'I don't care' – these people were for the most part friendly, happy, funny and supportive. A community that stuck up for itself and for each other. Gary didn't come from a home where he'd felt lost or rootless – he had security and safety, he got on with his parents, his brothers and sisters were only mildly irritating – but here in this room with no furniture and the thud thud thud thud thud of someone playing music far too loud upstairs, here were four solid walls where he could be who he wanted to be without having to argue or pretend. And without realising quite what he'd fallen into, here was a space where Gary could find his place in the world.

Upstairs in the room above his, someone was playing something loud and heavy. In the kitchen a boy and a girl were having an argument about cooking. On the front street, kids on cheap BMX bikes were shouting the odds at each other and laughing. Gary pulled on his running kit. A greying T-shirt he'd won at the Chew Valley race, a pair of shorts he'd been given for representing Yorkshire at cross-country, Walsh PB studded shoes, a tatty silver rain jacket and a peaked cap he'd been wearing almost continuously for the past month. And off he went, closing his door behind him, onto the Meanwood Trail, heading out, out, out towards the woods and the fields and the tracks and open space, slap-slap-slap feet on the hard soil.

CHAPTER 8

"You're off to great places! Today is your day! Your mountain is waiting – so get on your way!"

— Dr Seuss

In 1984 *The Fell Runner* magazine – an annual A5 typewritten handbook free to members of the Fell Running Association – announced details of a new British Junior Fell Running Championship. Taking a runner's best eight results from twelve races spread across the calendar, it reflected the growing number of teenagers interested in the sport. Juniors between 15 and 17 years old were encouraged to race, with the editorial stating, "It is hoped that clubs, schools, parents and senior runners will help Juniors get to races. There is much interest in Junior races but always a transport problem."

Gary had learned to drive in his dad's work van but now graduated to buying a battered yellow ex-British Telecom Ford Escort van for £250. The back of the van was a black hole that could be stuffed with runners, punks, tools, kit and dogs, sometimes all at the same time. Driving, Gary had worked out, was a good way to stay sober at a time when umpteen racing miles could have disappeared under a mountain of empty Pernod and cider bottles. Other than the booze, the squatting scene was also fuelled on speed, LSD and cannabis, none of which helped much with training schedules. For Gary, walking the thin line between elite athleticism and a culture of disengaged, drunken nihilism was an increasingly difficult place to be. Nevertheless, the mid-1980s were a time when Gary started to be noticed by the powers-that-be in charge of fell running. A good showing in the Junior Championships, alongside talented runners Micah Wilson and Robin Bergstrand, meant that the England team selectors chose Gary to represent England in the very first Junior World Mountain Racing Cup.

One of those on the selection committee was Norman Berry, an upright, eloquent and traditional runner who, after years of running with Holmfirth Harriers, became both Chairman of the Selection Committee and the Junior England team manager for the World Cup races. He was partnered with another veteran of the fells, Pete Bland – who, with a legacy of elite fell running behind him, had been forced through injury to stop racing and instead became part of the World Cup organising committee. These two were an unlikely pair – Bland the robust, plain-talking Northerner and Berry the well-spoken traditionalist – sharing a car on their way to pick up a couple of junior internationals on their way to the airport. They were flying to Morbegno in Italy for the first Junior World Cup races, and one of the two English Juniors picked was a runner that Norman hadn't yet met.

"In the car park, he said. In the service station car park."

Norman was in the passenger seat fiddling with a sheaf of A4 papers, plane times and contacts, plans and schedules, lists of runners, route maps, hotel details, dietary requirements, kit lists, telephone numbers.

Pete eyed the road signs and smiled. He was generally unflappable and calm, a solid counterpart to Norman's anxious attention to detail.

"Don't worry Norm. He'll be there."

"You've met the young chap haven't you? I mean I've seen his results. Splendid results. But I haven't met the lad."

Pete glanced sideways at Norman.

"Aye, I've met him. And you don't need to worry about recognising him."

"How do you mean?"

"Wait and see."

Pete's old Triumph slowed and pulled across to the inside lane, indicators flashing. The slip road to Hartshead Services was coming up and Norman was still shuffling through his papers. They pulled into the services and Pete slowed the car to a stop.

"There's the lad now Norm."

"Oh, right, where?"

"The one with the pink hair."

Norman's eyes widened as he fixed on a young lad walking towards them, a sloping, smirking jack-the-lad who was acknowledging that he'd seen Pete pulling up with the slightest nod of his head. He was dressed head-to-toe in black; black Doc Mart boots with the laces untied, black denim trousers with matching holes in the knees, a black T-shirt that once bore the name of a band but was by now just a jumble of assorted grey shapes and a black woollen cardigan that seemed to somehow hang on his torso as if it were a lazy animal, half-on and half-off, one sleeve measurably longer than the other. He had his kitbag slung over one shoulder and his hair was a dynamic, shocking pink. A specially-dyed-the-night-before pink. An "I'm running for England, look at me," pink.

Norman muttered, "Good God!"

"Told you we'd recognise him."

"Looks like he's been living on the street."

"Maybe he has. He can run though."

Norman composed himself as Pete got out of the car to take Gary's bag and swing it into the open boot. Norman, in the front, gave himself a talking-to. *Norman*, he said under his breath, *don't judge a book by its cover. Have you got that?*

Don't

judge

a

book

by

its

cover

!

!

!

!

Gary climbed into the back seat and greeted Norman with a quick smile. A brief handshake and Pete got in, started the engine, and headed to the airport and Italy.

The tentative and scary jump from juniors to seniors in any sport is always a crucial time. There are the physiological changes, the way growing bodies adapt to the increased stress on muscles, bones, tendons and ligaments. There's the stress of competing against better athletes and the anxiety that can come with increasing pressure to compete at a higher level. There's the added expectation that young athletes who've done well as juniors can continue to run faster, jump further, play better, hit harder, move quicker, think smarter, keep improving. And on top of all this are the added distractions of being a teenager – relationships, drink and drugs, friendship groups, music, fashion. All this happens at the same time as those teen hormones are wrestling inside their teen bodies to work out what comes next and why and when and how and why am I waiting so long and am I useless or does she fancy me or will I fail or a thousand things to think about other than, other than, other than –

Track pyramid sessions, every Tuesday and Thursday. Warm-up for 10-15 minutes, easy running and including dynamic stretching. Followed by:

2×400m high intensity with 200m recovery jog
1×800m high intensity with 400m recovery jog
1×1600m high intensity with 800m recovery jog
1×800m high intensity with 400m recovery jog
2×400m high intensity with 200m recovery jog
Cool-down for 10-15 minutes, easy running.

Gary had started competing in the senior fell races and doing well against the sport's top runners. The annual Winter Hill Fell Race was an 11-mile slog run early in the year around the Lancashire moor tops. With just under 3,000ft of climb, and run at the beginning of February, it was almost guaranteed to be freezing cold, cloudy and snowy underfoot. It was a place where the treacherous peat bogs from miles around came to play, sucking their early-season victims into the ground, chewing them up and then spitting them out. When Gary not only got round the tough course but finished third to winner Dave Cartridge it might have felt like a coming of age, had not Gary been putting in consistent results in these well-respected races for the past year – the steep, tough and craggy Fairfield Horseshoe in the Lake District (4th), the Burnsall Classic (short and rough, 3rd), Blackstone Edge in Lancashire (boggy, hilly and with an incredibly quick descent, 3rd) and Simon's Seat in the Yorkshire Dales (one of Gary's first senior victories).

All of which went to prove that the leap from junior to senior competitor – with all its attendant distractions – had barely affected Gary at all. The two quite separate halves of his life both appeared to be running on a shrug-your-shoulders, untroubled and carefree confidence that stemmed from *not fearing fear itself*. Of course things didn't always work out – sometimes he'd know he was having a bad race and would struggle to stay with runners he knew he should be beating – but if you've got the guts to go into Leeds city centre on a Saturday wearing bondage strapped trousers and a Mohican haircut then you've learned how to deal with fear. There's nothing wrong with being frightened – just don't let it stop you doing the things you want to do.

After Gary had first flown with the English Junior team to Italy he became for several years an on/off choice for both Junior, and then Senior, international races, the annual World Cup changing venue between European countries during those years. Most continental mountain races favoured the good climbers, often racing from bottom to top where they simply stopped – like a classic bike race, the runners were then ferried back to the finish below. This didn't favour Gary; British fell racing always included the descent, and it was in his downhill running that Gary knew he could beat most of his rivals. One particular International Junior race in France followed the continental pattern of two steep climbs with one short descent between them, finishing high above the start. One of Gary's rivals throughout his time as a fell-running junior, Robin Bergstrand – notable for racing in huge spectacles and headband – finished a brilliant second, while Gary came in 13th, helping the team to secure a second place. He was a little disappointed, but still, he'd earned another England vest, trained with the team and proved to Norman and Pete that he wasn't some sort of lawless troublemaker.

Norman and Pete, as organisers, coaches and guardians of the young runners who'd been chosen to represent their country abroad, routinely met at the end of each trip to debrief, to identify any problems that may have been thrown up. It was decided and agreed (and minuted) by the pair that the most troubling part of dealing with the unorthodox-looking lad with the pink hair wasn't to do with attitude, demeanour or any kind of unruly punk temperament; it was Gary's vegetarianism. Forget the media portrayal of punk as a snarling, spitting affront to civilised society – how do we source, in a small-town continental hotel, a cooked breakfast without meat?

An old African proverb says that, "If you don't initiate your young men into the tribe, they will burn down the village." It's why societies have coming-of-age rituals and rites of passage, and it's also why so many outstanding young athletes disappear from their sport as they reach college age – they need to demonstrate their own sense of self, need to find out who they are in the wider world. But Gary? Gary had punk rock. Punk rock at its best was open, inclusive, broadening, educational and life-affirming. And punk rock teaches you: *Don't judge a book by its cover.*

CHAPTER 9

*"So you've been to school for a year or two, and you know
you've seen it all..."*
— Jello Biafra, 'Holiday in Cambodia'

Between its inception in 1976 and the Christmas on Earth Festival
in Leeds in 1981, punk had changed. It was born out of a mish-
mash of ideas that were centred on the politics of situationism and
anarchism, a reaction against the austere boredom of 1970s Britain, a
backlash against artistic over-indulgence; it quickly spread its wings
to become a triumph of do-it-yourself get-up-and-play inventiveness,
where anything goes (and most things went). By the turn of the decade
punk embraced everything from fey female trios singing about the
seaside to jangly guitar boys with floppy fringes to doomy bass-driven
raincoat bands to stark and ranty free-form jazzers to hardcore leather
'n' studs full-on rock 'n' rollers to uncompromising New York synth
duos to communal-living anarcho-pacifists with fuzzy guitars. Garage
punk, pop punk, crust punk, folk punk, glam punk, skate punk, noise
punk and everything in between punk. If it was on an independent
label and it moved, someone would call it punk.

Gary's version of punk, however, wasn't up for either spreading
its wings or being overly inventive. It was simple, direct, uncluttered
– and it echoed what he loved about running on the fells. No frills
music, no frills running. Look, there's a hill – run to the top and back
down again. Choose your own route. 1, 2, 3, 4, four chord riffs, verse
chorus verse chorus verse chorus end. The simplest of beats, soil
beneath your feet, no heart-rate monitor, no keyboard solos, no fancy

watch, no four-part harmonies. And it was all fun – direct, energising, down-to-earth fun.

There's a history of great fell runners discovering their speed and ability on the hills and mountains and then realising that fell running simply doesn't pay. You can't make a career out of it. The switch to running sponsored, prize-moneyed road races is tantalising. Gary grew up seeing some of the best fell runners of his generation moving to the roads; for some it was successful and for some it was painful, a reminder that road-running at the elite level can bring with it a litany of injuries. When PE teacher Terry Lonergan had suggested he try, as an obviously talented young teenager, switching from fells to the 3,000 metres steeplechase, Gary wasn't interested. "It's got jumps and a bit of water. But it's still just going round and round a synthetic track."

A Thursday night after a training session over at the nearby Otley Chevin – six repetitions of its notorious winding climb through thick forest – Jan called round to Gary's house in Woodhouse bearing a gift of two cans of lager in a plastic carrier bag. Jan had heard about Gary's mum and dad splitting up, knew that it might be a strange and tough time for Gary, but that's not why he was calling round.

"Gary."

"Jan. How y'doing?"

"Good, yeah."

"Come in."

Jan walked in and saw that Gary's dog Sheba had been moved in from the old family home, and had taken up residence on the one armchair. There was a small portable TV on a pile of *The Fell Runner* magazines at the foot of the bed, a coat-hanger aerial twisted into its guts and forming a diamond-shape above the screen. It was switched on, but Jan couldn't make out what the programme was – something with cops in it. On the bed sat a girl, clothed in black from head to foot and with stark white make-up. He recognised her from somewhere, from a gig, from a squat, he couldn't remember. He waited for Gary to say something.

Awkward pause.

"Oh yeah right. This is Zombie."

Jan nodded.

"Zombie, this is Jan, my cousin. Well, my half-cousin."

Jan realised he couldn't sit on Sheba's armchair or plonk himself down on the bed next to Zombie. He stood there with that half-smile on his face, the one he wore at all times, disarming, friendly and approachable. On the TV now there were people talking about money-laundering, and he wondered what Zombie's real name might be. He wasn't going to ask. Sue. Helen. Nancy. Rachel. Anne. Kate. Sharon. Debbie. Lisa. Sarah –

Gary broke the silence.

"You got a room somewhere?"

"Yeah. Me and my girlfriend, we're over in Harold Avenue, there was a room. Near the Royal Park."

Gary and Jan hadn't talked properly since Jan had turned up to find that Gary had moved into his room at the squat. Jan shuffled from foot to foot and then remembered what he'd come round for.

"Here, I brought you a couple of cans," he said, by way of introduction, "and I had an idea. Me and Stu, we're still looking for a bass player, and –

"Yeah, I remember. That was absolutely ages ago. Haven't you found anyone mad enough or what?"

"No. Well, maybe."

"Maybe you've found someone?"

"Yeah."

"Go on."

"You."

"Me?"

"Yeah you."

"What? To play bass? You're joking."

"No. We've got a name now. Pagan Idols."

"Pagan Idols? Oh."

"Good name innit?"

"It's alright. What does it mean?"

"It's from a book I was reading. About how people used to worship these stone statues and things. Before Christianity. Just sounded good."

"Right."

"What do you reckon?"

"Erm… the bass guitar is the one with not as many strings, isn't it?"

"Yeah. There's only four. It's a lot easier than the guitar."

There was another pause.

"Are you asking me 'cos you know I can drive and I've got access to my dad's van?"

"No! Course not." (He was.)

"Where would I get a bass guitar?"

"I could try and borrow one. They're not that expensive. I think Ron Tree might have a spare one he can lend us."

Ron Tree was a legendary figure in Leeds. He played bass and did a lot of drugs. Not in that order – he did a lot of drugs and occasionally played bass. He built robots out of discarded junk he found on his stoned walks around Leeds 6. He pieced objects together, wired in lights and sound, then invited people round to take acid, listen to Hawkwind records and look at the robots. He was in a band called Bastard. Bastard were an uncompromisingly loud trio who played fast punk and Motorhead covers.

"Right. Well, ask him. I could have a go I suppose. What kind of music is it?"

Gary had heard a cassette of Jan and drummer Stu practising but that was six months ago. He needed reassurance that they were still playing straight-ahead punk rock and hadn't branched out into something esoteric like pop punk or crust punk or folk punk or glam punk or any other kind of punk other than just punk.

"It's punk. You've heard that cassette. We've only practised about three times since then. We've got a new song though. It's called 'Seeing Through Your Ruined Eyes.' It's got a phaser pedal on the guitar that Stu nicked from a student band. Sounds mental."

"Is Stu still a bit of a fascist?"

"A bit, yeah. But he's a good drummer."

"OK then. Ask Ron if he's got a bass I can borrow."

"You'll need an amp."

"An amp? Oh. Right."

"And a lead."

Gary realised that the longer Jan stayed, the more this was going to cost him. Where would he get an amp? What do you do with a lead? Did he want to be in a band? He didn't even know if he had a sense of rhythm, never mind play an instrument. But what he knew about was punk, and he knew that if punk had taught him anything it was 'Do it.' Punk – specifically Malcolm McLaren, its prime originator – had done the work of translating philosophers like Friedrich Nietzsche, by converting his dictum 'make a life, not a living' into the catch-all 'get off your arse, follow your desires and do what you want.' Rules? There were no rules. He thought back to his first real fell race, as a 12-year-old, up to the top of Ilkley Moor and back against a bunch of local school kids. One of them was Richard Nerurkar, who was already an international junior and tipped for a senior place in the Olympics. On the start line, everyone was talking about Nerurkar, about how he was going to win by a mile. Gary refused to be cowed, even in his first proper race. He set off too fast, half-killed himself on the climb to stay with the more experienced runner, and then overtook him on the descent. Get off your arse, follow your desires, do what you want. He didn't want to be a quantity surveyor, he wanted to be in a band. Who cared if this thought had only occurred to him in the last five minutes, with Jan turning up and basically buying his services as a bass player with two cans of lager? It didn't matter. What mattered now was finding a bass guitar and working out how to tune it.

As Gary settled into his life in the Leeds squatters' scene, he gradually developed a routine that suited both his life in:

1) the subterranean world of punk, centred around gigs, parties, alcohol, irresponsibility, drugs, relationships, fights, dole money, distraction, fanzines, records, fun, late nights, friendships and fall-outs; and

2) the ongoing world of fell running, centred around training runs, races, focus, commitment, dedication, blah blah blah (he didn't get very far with this half of the list).

The balancing act between the two sides of his life might have been easier were it not for his current club – Skyrac AC – being out in Guiseley, ten miles away from the Leeds 6 epicentre of the Punk World As He Knew It. Inevitably, Gary started to think about changing running clubs. The closest club geographically was the all-powerful Leeds City AC, mainly populated by students and ex-students, road and track runners, usually immaculately turned-out and superbly-organised. They had a team of qualified coaches, their own track and over 400 members. They were scary. Gary was running for Skyrac mainly because his brother Bradley and his mate Tim Agar ran there. It was a good club, a friendly club, a local club. But, like Leeds City, it wasn't a fell running club. There was another reason to find a club close to his new home: since the bath at the squat was pretty much always in need of repair, he needed somewhere to have a twice-weekly shower without driving out to his mum or dad's house.

Richard Pallister, his friend from St Mary's, had recently joined Pudsey & Bramley, an old club that met and trained at Priesthorpe School, halfway between Leeds and Bradford. *Go on then Richard, sell 'em to me.* For starters, they had a better-looking vest than

Skyrac. Maroon with a gold diagonal stripe, a proper old style design. Secondly, they had Pete Watson. Pete was getting on a bit but was a proper legend in fell running, having won the Burnsall Classic race several times in the 1960s. Thirdly, there was Jack Maitland, British Fell Champion in 1986 and a pioneer of the idea of fell running as a sort of itinerant lifestyle, something which obviously appealed to Gary.

Pudsey & Bramley began life in a dilapidated wooden hut in the middle of a rutted, patchy sports field in 1910. Back then – and for around fifty years – they were known as Bramley & District Harriers, heavy-vested track & field athletes with names like Cliff Thorpe and Frank Christmas. Really. Bramley is an industrial area of Leeds, situated well away from the more affluent university-based runners and the famous Leeds City Athletics club as well as the (even back at the beginning of the twentieth century) towering presence of big noisy neighbours, Bingley Harriers. Gary already knew about Bingley Harriers; he'd enjoyed his time there and knew he'd benefitted from the competition, but he was, when all's said and done, Leeds.

Bramley's Albert Swainson was one of the first to get involved in competitive racing on the Yorkshire hills, winning the Burnsall Fell Race four times in the 1930s – a connection between the club and that short, sharp up-and-down race that endured through the years. Albert's trailblazing inspired a generation of Bramley runners gathering in their little wooden hut, not least two local lads named Alan Cocking and Pete Watson. It was the '50s, and these two spent the next decade or two racing, and winning, on the Yorkshire fells. Cocking had an England vest as a cross-country runner, while Watson became famous for winning those successive Burnsall Fell Races.

The club officially became Pudsey & Bramley AC around 1961, when a local Bramley builder bought both hut and playing field, forcing the club to move into Pudsey (still half a marathon's distance from a proper fell) where it gradually gathered a new crop of runners, inspired in turn by Pete Watson's victories. Jack Maitland, a refugee from Edinburgh now living in Leeds, took on the maroon-and-gold mantle mainly because, as a student, he could get lifts to races. Jack's modus operandi during the first half of the 1980s had a healthy dollop of punk attitude about it; he lived from race to race, took part-time work in a running shoe shop, never drove and always scrounged lifts to and from races, often basing his choice of his next race entirely on someone offering a lift to somewhere close. He carried a sleeping bag in his running kit and would sleep anywhere if it fit with his running. He ran every day, and tried to race at least twice a week, every week – any kind of competition would do (track, cross-country, road, triathlon), though he would always prefer a fell or mountain race.

Jack was everywhere, his small frame and wide grin belying a serious and determined competitiveness. During what many people see as fell running's heyday, when John Wild and Kenny Stuart were battling head-to-head in all the major races and breaking records, Jack was just behind them, nipping at their heels and probably asking if they could give him a lift to an upcoming race in Scotland, Wales or the Lakes.

"Well… I can fit you in the car Jack, but where will you stay?"

"On your living room floor, whatever."

"But the dog sleeps in the living room."

"I don't mind sharing."

Jack was also one of the first British fell runners to race on the continent, hitching his way from alpine race to alpine race, living off his prize winnings and somehow keeping up a rigorous and punishing training regime. His happy-go-lucky nomadic wanderings were as much part of his running as the races he won and the records he broke. It became the Pudsey & Bramley way – a carefree and easygoing attitude to the sport linked to a fierce competitiveness and an almost reckless lack of responsibility and restraint.

Gary was sold. A new floor to sleep on, a new club to run for.

It was claimed by a handful of London-based cultural commentators that punk was already dead and buried by 1978. The Sex Pistols, their bass player a confirmed heroin addict, had imploded at the end of a gig in San Francisco with Johnny Rotten's famous last words, "Ever get the feeling you've been cheated?" The cultural phenomenon that had burned so brightly seemed, arguably, to have flickered out within a couple of short, dazzling years.

Outside of the capital, it didn't happen like that at all. What may have been a flash of inspired chaos that detonated a bomb beneath the lazy arses of the national media became a slowly-spreading wave of do-it-yourself creativity that grew into a nationwide punk movement, spearheaded by a bunch of ex-hippy squatters in Epping, just outside London. This bunch of maverick performance artists, calling themselves Crass, saw that initial burst of punk energy as a clarion call and began to make their own version of Malcolm McLaren's "anyone can do it" dictum into something inspiring, a set of ideas based not just on loud, fast music but on a way of living, on pacifist, anarchist, feminist politics.

They courted controversy, got banned, made records that were discussed in Parliament and turned a generation of young punk kids on to the idea that punk wasn't a fashion but a way of life. Crass spearheaded a move away from the King's Road clothes shops and towards a sustainable way of self-organising. Right across the country, teenagers were inspired to set up concerts, write and print fanzines, create activist groups, start food co-operatives, squat empty houses, grow their own food, protest against Thatcher's austerity and warmongering and co-ordinate community action.

For a short while, Gary wore his leather jacket emblazoned with

Crass symbols, painted with a tin of Dulux white satin finish. He didn't paint it himself – there was a lad who lived over at Richmond Terrace who was good at painting, and he'd gladly paint whatever band logos or peace signs you wanted on your jacket for a few smokes or cans. The Richmond Terrace squat was notorious and had the nickname 'Sillyville' – it rose out of a garden full of discarded electrical appliances, kitchen utensils, mattresses and bike frames, a tall, red-brick terrace that was owned by an absentee landlord who'd escaped abroad during a court case about his finances. Someone got hold of the list of properties that the landlord had left behind, and as the students moved out of them at the end of their time at Leeds University and Polytechnic, the squatters moved in.

Sillyville housed up to twelve people at a time, sleeping on floors, landings and sofas. Every night someone would cook up a huge pot of stew on the old enamel gas stove and people would emerge from their rooms, often having just woken up, for a big communal meal. Vegetarian, of course. Let's hear it for Nut, Wisey, Rufflebar Dave, Squatter Dave, (there were two Daves so they had to have extra names), Bod, Pete, Dev, Havoc... The house was just a few doors from another communal house occupied by a band called Little Chief, all dreadlocks, dope and smiles; they'd spend long summer evenings playing music in their front garden. Everyone was either on the dole or on a Youth Training Scheme, working as apprentices for a pittance and spending it all on cans of Special Brew and hash.

On the highest crockery shelf in the kitchen, up at the top with the chipped mixing bowls and pan lids, was the Pluto cup, an ordinary-looking teacup bearing an image of Disney's canine character wearing a green collar and cocking one ear upwards, a bone hanging out of its mouth. The Pluto cup had been discovered abandoned underneath the bed when Vegan Tony had hurriedly left his room at the house one summer, leaving most of his possessions behind and heading off to the continent in a green Citroen 2CV known as 'the tin snail'. The Pluto cup was half-full of very stale urine. Instead of simply throwing the cup away, it was rinsed out and kept on the top shelf and reserved for special visitors. Every year or so there'd be cause for the police to call round, usually as a result of some minor shop-lifting offence or simply to keep tabs on who was coming and going… come in officer, have a seat, and (inevitably…) would you like a cup of tea?

Gary's Crass jacket didn't last long – the combination of peace signs and anarchist politics felt too serious, too po-faced and thought-out. Crass's extreme music, all harsh guitars and barked, tuneless vocals spat out at a million miles per hour, spawned a thousand imitators, bands made up of out-of-school and out-of-work punks (almost all boys, of course) playing their instruments faster and louder and angrier than Crass and screaming about the threat of nuclear war and about animal experiments and police violence and the surveillance state and Ronald Reagan and love and peace and freedom and anarchy, all so blurringly fast that the words were lost in a machine-gun jumble of syllables and spit. Where Crass had been articulate and reasoned, the next generation – the wayward children they spawned – were confrontational, their watchword being the title of a song by a band from London called DIRT (Death Is Reality Today):

Object
Refuse
Reject
Abuse

Gary's was the generation that missed the Sex Pistols and the Clash, and their aim seemed to be to out-punk their predecessors. They wanted nothing more than to be faster, louder, uglier, scarier, angrier, more intimidating, more outraged, more splenetic, more raucous, more violently, rabidly, impetuously fierce. The Leeds punks would meet at the bar on Leeds train station, crawling out of the suburban woodwork, gathering in the one place that sold beer early and late, that didn't have local customers, that smelt of the toilets that everyone used (to avoid paying for the station toilets), that rattled and rang with one-arm bandits. From there they'd leave in bunches, heading for one of the regular punk venues: Brannigans, Adam & Eve's, the Bierkeller, the 1 in 12 Club. If there wasn't a band on there'd be punk records playing, so it was always too loud to talk and too loud to think. This was Gary's world, a repeating pattern of noise and alcohol. At least, that's what the rest of the punks thought.

The only sign in Gary's room that he was by now an international athlete was a small collection of cups and trophies that he lined up on the floor in the corner near his kitbag. There was a photograph of him standing with his new Pudsey & Bramley club members, all in their maroon and yellow vests, at the start of a race. It wasn't framed, just propped up on the mantlepiece next to a clock that didn't work and a neat line of VHS video cassettes (he didn't have a video player). The other people in his house rarely saw him coming and going (they by and large kept different hours) and although they had an idea that he was a runner – or at least, that he went out running – they couldn't, and didn't, know the extent of it. Word got around fairly quickly that Gary had a small van, and still had access to his dad's bigger van and that he was happy to drive people to out-of-town gigs. In effect this meant seeing how many punks could squeeze into one box-shaped space while having enough arm-room to drink from two-litre bottles of cider and smoke endless spliffs. Gary would be sober, at the wheel, happy to head off to Nottingham or Bradford or Wakefield with a howling, yelling, coughing and occasionally vomiting bunch of punks crow-barred into the back.

Jan's band, Pagan Idols, now with Gary on bass, began rehearsing in the basement at Gary's dad's house. Hughie was planning on moving, but for now he rattled around the old place with Bradley, the house's reputation as a hive of family gatherings now sadly forgotten.

It was a trek out to Ilkley but there was a basement and Hughie was happy to let them make as much noise as they wanted, providing it didn't interfere with:

1) *Eastenders*

2) *Tomorrow's World*

or

3) any televised sporting event. *Any*. Wrestling, horse-racing, football, rugby, golf, snooker, cricket, athletics. Especially athletics. Since Gary and his brother Bradley had both turned their backs on Hughie's beloved rugby league in order to concentrate on running, Hughie had become obsessive about athletics, about track & field and cross-country, loving his trips to various town and village showgrounds to watch Gary competing in top-level mountain races.

"That's my lad, that one there."

"Which one?"

"The one over on the left. With the maroon vest."

"The one with the daft hair?"

"That's the one."

The band was shaping up, and Gary bought a second-hand bass from Manning's Musicals in Bradford – a Squier Fender copy, sunburst finish, new set of strings and strap thrown in – for £75. The shop was run by a bloke called Malcolm, an ex-circus performer who'd travelled all round Europe as a trombone-playing clown, and who'd settled into a life surrounded by used guitars, faulty amplifiers and dented brass instruments. His policy was, price 'em high, then let yourself be knocked down, tenner by tenner, until you reached a compromise that was still above what the instrument was worth but meant the buyer thought he'd got a bargain. Everyone wins. Gary liked it, the bass, liked the way you could sling it low, low, low, just high enough to be able to reach all four strings with a plectrum. It had a weight to it, it could root you, ground you, solid and heavy and holding the sound together between the drums and the guitar. Gary figured he'd never be a great player, but it meant he was IN A BAND. Not just following bands or listening to bands or buying records by bands or jumping up and down at Adam & Eve's to bands but actually, factually, really and honestly IN A BAND.

It was the middle of the 1986 European Athletics Championships in Stuttgart and Hughie was holding out for some silence so he could watch the 1500 metres final in the comfort of his living room. Bradley was slumped beside him, sticking Panini Mexico World Cup football stickers into a book. Julio Romero, Paraguay. Bruno Conti, Italy. Luis Fernandez, France. British middle-distance legend Seb Coe had already won the 800 metres gold medal a few days earlier, beating his younger rival Steve Cram into third place. Hughie didn't like Coe, he was too nice, too clean, too perfect. He was well-spoken, a daddy's boy, short hair and immaculate kit. Cram was different, he was the kid with the long wavy hair, with a Jarrow accent, he was a northerner, working class, and he could laugh, too. Hughie had one tense hand wrapped around a glass of whiskey and one tense hand on the arm of his chair, his Telefunken colour set doing battle with the Pagan Idols, Gary, Jan, Stu and Tom in the cellar, thumping and shouting and clanging and humming, a furious stop-start practice, the same song over and over and over again. Normally Hughie would be loving the lads making their bloody racket, chuckling and pouring another whiskey and laughing at how the dogs retreated upstairs and whimpered at the crash bang screech of it all. Not tonight. Coe and Cram. Cram and Coe. Here we go. Big build-up. He was poised and ready to yell at the band to switch off for ten minutes when they fell silent. Both Hughie and Bradley held their breath in hope. Silence. It's on. Let's go.

Downstairs, the band had stopped for a cig break – Stu was unable to get through more than a handful of songs without needing a cigarette – and Jan was talking ten-to-the-dozen, kneeling on the threadbare carpet that had been resurrected from the backyard shed and was supposed to absorb some of the punky noise (but didn't). He had news. Important news that he'd been saving.

"Right, listen. We've got a gig!"

"Seriously? Where?"

"At a squat they're opening up in Leeds."

"Who's opening it up?"

"The Chumbas lot. You know the White Cloth Hall, behind the Corn Exchange? Big old empty building? Well they've been inside, got in through the roof. They're going to open it as a squat all-dayer, loads of bands on."

"I hate Chumbas."

"Me too."

"Yeah but it's a gig."

"Right. Yeah. Great. When?"

"Dunno yet. It's a secret."

"How do you mean it's a secret?"

"We get told a week before, and put word round. They can't advertise it or tell anyone before that, 'cos the building will get secured if the cops find out."

Stu and Gary were excited but trying not to show it. Tom, the drummer, fiddled with his sticks, drew on his cig and couldn't have been less excited. He hit a cymbal, which stopped the conversation dead, its decaying sizzle emptying into a near-silence. Tom wasn't quite sure why he was in this band, with its anti-war song titles and Jan's lyrics and Gary's jacket and Stu's hair. Tom was a skinhead, he wanted to be in a tough band like Sham 69 or Cockney Rejects, a band that got into fights and sang about football. Instead he was stuck with the cider-drinking, laughing, pogoing, speed-snorting punks. Jan carried on and from the room upstairs they could hear the telly, hear a sports commentary, hear Hughie's feet as he rose from his armchair. Then a loud roar –

"Yeeeeeaaasssssssssss!"

Gary looked at Stu, Stu looked at Jan, Jan looked puzzled. Gary spoke.

"Steve Cram must've won. My dad hates Seb Coe."

Tom didn't understand a word. He threw his drum sticks across the room, stubbed his cigarette out on a cymbal and folded his arms in a sulk.

Two weeks later, on a drizzly Saturday afternoon, Gary's van pulled up outside the old White Cloth Hall. They'd been told to get there early, and it was now mid-afternoon. They weren't onstage until 6pm, which meant plenty of drinking time – though with Gary driving, he'd be staying sober. The front doors to the building were closed and it was all suspiciously quiet. A sign was sellotaped to the door above a letterbox that was nailed shut.

Section 6 of the Criminal Law Act states that there are people living in this property who claim a legal right to be here. Anyone – even the actual owner of the property – who tries to enter the building without lawful permission will be committing an offence.

Jan knocked on the door.

"Hello? Is anyone there?"

A voice from inside shouted, "Who is it?"

"It's Jan, from Pagan Idols."

"Oh hiya Jan, this is Zippy. Have you got your stuff?"

"Yeah."

"I can't let anyone in this entrance, can you go round the back? There's a gate with a padlock on but just shout there and someone'll let you in. You might have to climb the fence."

"But we've got a drum kit."

"Well, chuck that over first and someone will catch it."

Inside the hall were around 100 punks, gathered in small groups, some sitting on the dusty floor and some idling around tables that had been set up to sell books and pamphlets. There were no chairs, just occasional wooden crates and some empty musical equipment boxes that people had commandeered. The large room, one side all windows and the rest all peeling paint, smelt musty and redundant. It hadn't been in use for two decades and was a listed building, its long central hall once a place where textile traders would measure, sample, buy and sell cloth and fabric. The audience had to enter by climbing a high fence and answering questions asked from behind a closed iron door. Who are you? Who are you with? The day-long event was a benefit to raise money for a local women's shelter; all the bands were playing for free. There was no stage, just an area at one end of the hall with a small vocal PA, some drums and a few amplifiers. Having spent an hour discussing where they could get hold of a generator, the punks who'd broken into the building were surprised to find that the electricity supply could be turned on with a single switch in the building's damp and dingy cellar.

Pagan Idols' first proper gig – proper meaning not just playing to your mates in your dad's basement or in someone's bedroom at the Richmond Terrace squat, without drums – consisted of seven songs, two of them played twice, and a lot of out-of-tune and out-of-time chaos. Jan got nervous and drank far too much before they played, and remembered too late that he'd left all his crib sheets, with the guitar chords written in black marker really big so he could see them when they were taped to the floor, in a Tesco carrier bag in Gary's room.

Lead singer Stu, tall and awkward, wearing two black leather studded belts criss-crossing his waist and a white shirt with the sleeves ripped off, forgot the words to most of the songs, instead repeating lines over and over. Tom's drums, in the concrete-floored space of the old Cloth Hall with its iron pillars and bare walls, sounded a hundred times louder than they usually did in Hughie's cellar, every snare-crack and tom-boom echoing around the venue. Consequently, both Gary and Jan struggled spectacularly to keep in time and the resulting noise sounded like one of Jan's hardcore punk cassettes playing backwards. The band played in front of a banner that depicted a cartoon face which could have been a pig or a devil or just a drunk punk, and under the spray-painted face was the slogan

ADMIT YOUR FUCKED

When they'd finished, applauded by 30 or 40 punks who kept faith through the whole set, Gary packed away his bass into its case and threw it into the back of the van along with Jan's guitar, two amps, all the disassembled pieces of the drum kit and Jan, Stu, Tom, Nut, Cardigan, Damien and Zombie. He was sober and happy and, after spending two hours driving around Leeds depositing people and equipment to their homes, he was home by 2am and could sleep looking forward to tomorrow morning's easy run along the Meanwood Valley to Eccup Reservoir, flat and fast. But not too fast – the day after was the Simon's Seat race, one of his favourites, a race he'd run previously in both Bingley and Skyrac colours. Now he would be in his new Pudsey & Bramley vest – he hadn't even worn it enough for it to look, like the rest of his kit, faded, grubby, crumpled and torn – and he wanted to win.

Racing as a junior, he expected to finish in the top handful; and winning was, if not commonplace, then at least hardly a surprise. Junior courses were often shorter than the senior races, which suited Gary – he was still learning the mountaincraft that was essential to compete with the long-distance experts in the long, Category 'A' races. The Coniston fell race – a brutal 12-mile course with 3,000 feet of climb, taking in the summits of Wetherlam and Swirl How before climbing to Coniston Old Man and descending along loose and hazardous stone tracks – was an early test of the harder mountain races. The previous year, Gary had finished in 10th place, around two or three minutes behind the leaders Shaun Livesey and Dave Cartridge. These were all names he knew he'd have to compete with now, names that had dominated the sport for several years, and he knew, too, that being able to compete over the tough, long races didn't come naturally, it came with this race-by-race experience. This year, Gary improved his position in the Coniston race, finishing in third place, only three seconds behind winner Billy Bland, having kept in touch with Bland's incredible descending speed from the final summit down to the finish.

Gary was steadily acquiring that mountaincraft: knowledge of terrain, ability with a map and compass, long-lasting strength and stamina, understanding when to take on water, when to eat, knowing where to make an effort and where to relax. The Lake District runners, especially those competing for Keswick AC and Ambleside AC, ran those mountains and those distances week in, week out. They lived and worked among the peaks and valleys, not in a squatted house in the middle of Leeds.

Simon's Seat, a great moorland outcrop in the Yorkshire Dales topped with crags, was known as a place of magic – there were rumours of Neolithic and Bronze Age sites and tales of druidic worship on the rocks at its summit. In the early spring rain, and with the wind whipping around the higher slopes, it looked distinctly un-magical, its long dominant shape fading into the low, heavy cloud. At its foot, the stony path wound down to the River Wharfe and the ribbon of road that led westwards to Appletreewick, a tiny hamlet bookended by two pubs. A long line of parked cars edged the road and runners were heading up to a farm at the bottom of the hill, where race organisers had cleared a space to write out entry forms and collect the £1.50 entry fee. The barn smelled, naturally, of cow shit, but the rain was forcing runners to use it for shelter, chatting and stretching and laughing and pinning and re-pinning race numbers onto their vests. The route would leave the large field adjacent to the barn and head part-way up the walkers' track leading up the hill, before branching off onto a smaller, peat 'n' rocks path heading for the summit. Once at the top, runners had to clamber across the stony outcrop before hurtling off the west side of the hill, half a mile downwards and then a sharp turn to climb diagonally back to rejoin the track leading back to the farm. It wasn't the toughest of races, but the loose, rocky surface made it tricky, turned it into a battle with your own self-confidence, your own approach to danger – which is exactly what Gary loved. He knew that there were a handful of runners who could outsprint him, but he knew that a descent like this was about fearlessness, throwing caution to the open moorland wind, disregarding the voice that tells you to slow, to take care, to watch your step.

Lining up alongside Gary in the steep, muddy and rainswept field were two of the sport's current stars, Shaun Livesey and Jack Maitland. Both were battling to be 1986's British fell running champion of the year, both had a pedigree of class and experience, and neither was prepared to be beaten by the peroxided, tattooed teenager in the scruffy kit, the kid with the Mohican haircut, the hair that lay wilted to one side in the rain like a mop that needed to be wrung. Nerves play a part in racing, even when you're an established winner – it was important to look confident, relaxed, ready for anything. Elite runners would jog casually away from the start line minutes before the starting whistle was blown, off in their own worlds, giving nothing away. Don't show weakness; if it was raining, wear only a vest. Focus. Gary's way was different – his way was to joke, to laugh, to take the piss, to nudge and elbow and jostle, to look like he could be in a social gathering anywhere, anywhere except for the start line of a hill race, to look like he was in the queue at Adam & Eve's drinking from a flask of Pernod, waiting to see Icons of Filth or Napalm Death or Crucifix or Hagar the Womb.

There was another thing: Gary had grown up doing a lot of his long training runs out here, Saturday morning training runs that started with being dropped off by his dad at Bolton Abbey before heading up Desolation Valley to the moorland top at Simon's Seat and on to a winding up and down route across to Barden Reservoir and around the summit monument above Cracoe before descending to his auntie's house at Airton. Pant, pant, pant. All across the area there were historic fell race routes, many of them professional races, and Gary had raced all of them from a young age. Since the official visit from the Northern Counties representative he'd held off running in any of the non-amateur competitions, but he was aware that the tide was turning in the division between professional and amateur, and more runners were questioning the system whereby running up a hill under one athletic code could get you banned from running up a hill under another. Simon's Seat could have been a classic professional race, a single summit, open fell and a finish next to a barn in a farmer's field.

Gary was still making jokes and put-downs as the starter blew a whistle and the couple of hundred runners set off up the steep field towards an open five-bar gate. By the time they'd climbed through a strip of forest and emerged at the foot of the fell proper, Gary was together with Jack and Shaun and turning to ascend alongside a high stone wall. Jack was the better climber of the three, Gary the better descender; but it was Shaun who began to push ahead as they gained height up towards the summit. Jack began to fall away as Shaun and Gary clambered up around the white-painted trig point perched above the wide valley. There was no sinking evening sun, just a hazy gauze thrown across the north of England, the vibrant summer colours of the land paling to a collection of dingy greens.

The descent off the top was where Gary made his move, leaping over loose boulders, gambling and taking risks with footholds and knowing that Shaun would be more careful, more wary, more calculating, less cavalier, less risky. By the time they reached the wall which signalled a left turn and a climb back up to the summit ridge, Gary was ten, fifteen seconds in front and knew that he had to hold onto the gap as he huffed and heaved up the thin, muddy track beside the wall. Reaching the skyline he could hear Shaun's heavy breathing behind him, gradually closing, step by step and breath by breath. But it was too late – Gary turned on to the descending path still in the lead and knew then that he had the race won. It took only a handful of minutes to cover the steep and treacherously bouldered route back down to the forest, into the finishing field and, with a backward glance to make sure, an easy run to the line. The gap had opened to around thirty seconds and Gary had proved he could race, and win, against the best runners in the country. He stood with his hands on his hips, watching as Shaun Livesey sprinted down the field to finish, watching as Jack Maitland came in another thirty seconds after that, watching as both regained their breath, watching and waiting for the chance to say, with that slightly crooked and broad smile, "What took you two so long?"

L–R: Gary (age 6), Bradley, Lynne & Maureen.

St Mary's Catholic High School, Menston, age 12.

Local BOFRA race winner. The GB tracksuit is from representing GB Catholics in a European cross-country race.

Gary and his dad Hughie at Gotts Park, Leeds, after an inter-schools race.

Bradley and Gary in matching outfits as Jan (centre) and his brother Andi (left) come to visit.

Gary aged fifteen in a Bingley Harriers vest.

Pagan Idols after a gig in Holbeck, Leeds – Stu, Gary, Jan.

Pagan Idols: Gary on bass, Tom on drums, Stu on vocals, Jan on guitar.

Pudsey & Bramley van on European tour, 1988. Gary tries to secure kit bags to the roof while Scoffer looks on.

The England men's World Cup team, Keswick, 1988. L–R, back row: Dave Cartridge, Malcolm Patterson, Gary. Front row: Rod Pilbeam, Paul Dugdale, Ray Owen, Robin Bergstrand. Sean Livesey has gone AWOL.

The Pudsey & Bramley men's team, Ben Nevis, 1989. L–R, back row: Boff Whalley, Pete Bullen, Ady Illingworth, Gary Devine, Mike Falgate, Richard Pallister. Front row: Danbert Nobacon, Alan Greenwood, Brian Stevenson.

Gary, Jan & Stu at a squat in Bradford.

Gary and Jan in front of Hughie's white van.

Gary, sporting a black eye, descending to victory at Simon's Seat fell race, 1989. (Photo: Eileen Woodhead)

Gary running at the Mountain Running World Cup, Keswick, 1988.
(Photo: Peter Hartley)

CHAPTER 10

1990 British Championship race 3
Ennerdale Horseshoe Race, 23rd June 1990
23 miles, 7500ft climb

"We do not belong to those who only get their thought from books, or at the prompting of books – it is our custom to think in the open air, walking, leaping, climbing or dancing on lonesome mountains by preference…"
— Nietzsche

One of the Lakeland classics, the Ennerdale Horseshoe, was essentially a long and narrow loop of a series of classic Cumbrian mountains, reading from start to finish like a high-level Stations of the Cross:

Great Bourne
Red Pike
Green Gable
Kirk Fell
Pillar
Haycock
Iron Crag
Crag Fell

A hellish series of climbs and descents with only one water source, at Black Beck Tarn around the halfway point, made this race for many a matter of survival. In hot weather it was a battle to stay hydrated and in wet weather simply a battle to stay upright. In 1981 a runner named Bob English went off course in poor weather and fell badly, being discovered unconscious and with head injuries. He died while being taken to hospital.

Not Gary's kind of race at all in fact, its attritional ruggedness and emphasis on navigation playing into the hands of the older, more experienced Lakeland runners who spent their days rounding up sheep and their evenings drinking pints of cows' blood before knocking off thirty or forty training miles over England's highest peaks wearing only their work boots. But a Championship race was a Championship race, and Colin Donnelly was doing it, and Mark Rigby and Gary's fast-improving club team-mate Paul Sheard were doing it, and there were important points at stake, and it could mean the difference between winning and losing the Championship, and it was only 23 miles and, and, and –

And the phone in the hallway rang. The phone in the hallway that sat on the thick wedge of the Yellow Pages phone directory on the bare wooden floor and never rang. And when it did ring, nobody answered it. It stopped ringing, and then rang again. Nobody appeared. When it stopped and rang a third time it was clearly someone who'd been told, "If you're ringing, try at least three times. Nobody answers it the first time."

Gary turned down his music ('Big A, Little A' by Crass. He hadn't played this single for donkey's years. It was brilliant – loud, shouty, inspiring) and wandered out to the hallway to pick up the annoying ringing thing and put it out of its misery.

"Hello."

"I'm ringing to talk to Gary Devine."

"That's me."

"Ah. Good, hello Gary –"

Gary tried to work out how many people he knew with the

well-spoken eloquence of the caller. The Queen's English, Received Pronunciation, BBC-speak. How many? Three, four, maybe five.

"It's Danny. Danny Hughes."

"Oh. Right. Hi."

Danny was a national representative on various official bodies governing Europe-wide fell and mountain running. In all official matters, Danny would normally phone up a club president or secretary; in the case of Pudsey & Bramley, nobody was quite sure who was in charge of what, so Gary would have to do.

"What it is Gary, you see, is that the IMRF*, who were formerly the ICMR*, have been in touch to invite the leading clubs from each participant country's Association, in our case the FRA* through the AAA* and of course the IAAF*, to send a team to compete in Italy in three weeks' time."

"Erm…"

"And to cut a long story short, with Pudsey & Bramley being last year's team champions, that invitation goes to your club. Your best three runners representing England in a mountain relay-race in the hills of Tuscany. All accommodation and flights paid for. Your chance to compete in the 27th Trofeo Terza Punta Monte Morello."

"Sounds alright."

"There is a problem, however – it's on the weekend of the Ennerdale Championship race."

Gary thought this through for two, three, four seconds.

"We get put up?"

"So I'm led to believe."

"And fed?"

"All in."

"Right. The answer's yes."

"Do you need time to consult the rest of the team?"

"No."

"Oh. Lovely. I'll let the organisers know we'll be accepting the invitation. I shall accompany you of course. All you need to do now is let me know which three runners will make up the team so that I can make the necessary arrangements. Can you let me know by tomorrow?"

"Yeah. No problem."

"Alright. Splendid. I'll give you a call tomorrow, same time."

"Right. If no-one answers, just keep ringing. Three times should do it."

Gary put down the phone and retreated to his record player. Lift the arm, pull it across, repeat play. 'Big A, Little A', Crass.

> *Be exactly who you want to be, do what you want to do*
> *I am he and she is she but you're the only you*
> *No one else has got your eyes, can see the things you see*
> *It's up to you to change your life and my life's up to me*
> *If the programme's not the one you want, get up, turn off the set*
> *It's only you that can decide what life you're gonna get…*

The 1980s was a high watermark in sport's history of mavericks and nonconformists. It seemed like people were getting tired of the mantras of stick to the rules, play by the book, go with the flow, follow the crowd, don't make waves, toe the line. For too long there had been an adherence to the Victorian distrust of the unorthodox, to the *Chariots of Fire* narrative which centred around Sir John Gielgud's Cambridge college master telling Harold Abrahams that sport is meant to be about the *"unassailable spirit of loyalty"*, that non-conformists, in the words of Gielgud's character, messed with *"esprit de corps"*. The 1980s, bankrolled and promoted by an increasingly huge international television audience, seized on the drama of sport, and there was nothing more dramatic than the rebels and insubordinates, those who refused to do as they were told, the renegades and rotters, bullies and underdogs, heroes and villains, drug-users and scrappers and spoilt brats, icons and iconoclasts. So in no particular order:

John McEnroe, repeatedly yelling, "You cannot be serious!" at umpire Edward James before swearing at tournament referee Fred Hoyles during Wimbledon 1981.

Zola Budd, barefoot middle- and long-distance runner from apartheid South Africa, running on after she trips adversary Mary Decker and leaves her sprawling on the track in the 1984 Olympics final.

Diego Maradona, punching the ball into the English goal at the World Cup Finals in 1986 before claiming with a wink that the goal was scored "by the hand of God".

Sebastian Coe, unable to contain his disgust at being offered a handshake by rival Steve Ovett following defeat in the Moscow Olympics 800 metre final.

Formula One driver Nelson Piquet, jumping from his car to confront and punch rival Eliseo Salazar after a crash in the 1982 German Grand Prix.

Australian fast bowler Dennis Lillee assaulting Pakistan captain Javed Miandad in the heated 1981 Test Match between the two countries.

Wimbledon FC, unfancied underdogs against Liverpool FC in the 1988 FA Cup Final, winding up their opponents in the pre-match tunnel with cries of 'Yidaho!' – an adapted mangling of the words 'in the hole', which was in turn short for the phrase, "Let's tear off their heads and shit in the hole."

The 1980s was a golden age of sporting drama that shook off much of the traditional niceties of 'esprit de corps' and gave sport the dramatic tension and eccentric caricatures of soap operas and Hollywood blockbusters. Fell running existed in a dark corner away from the more ridiculous excesses of professional sport, generally able to 'get on with it' in a spirit of self-management and communality. It was thought that the sport could never be televised

– lugging huge camera equipment to the summits of mountains only to see the runners appearing out of the mist, touching the trig point and then disappearing again – but nevertheless the sport had a barely-disguised tradition of post-race drunken antics that sometimes ended up either in the local papers or in the dock of the local court (and sometimes both). What Gary was discovering was that his punk ethos, the sweeping nihilism he'd taken on as a young teenager and which dictated everything from the way he lived and the clothes he wore to the food he ate and the music he listened to, chimed nicely with fell running's ethos of adventure and risk. It wasn't, as was the case in so many of professional sport's examples of bad-boy/girl behaviour, about winning at all costs or being a sore loser; it was about playing the game your own way, choosing your own path, escaping the rules and restrictions that surround you in the real, everyday, bog-standard, working, routine run-of-the-mill world and heading for a place of freedom and surprise. In essence, fell running was nonconformist, maverick, separatist… or possibly just plain weird.

*

Three members of Pudsey & Bramley AC convened in the Three Horseshoes pub, on the Otley Road, wondering why they were there. Or not so much wondering. They were there because Gary had suggested to them, quietly, that they should be there. The previous two hours had been spent at the old cinder track up by Lawnswood roundabout and a stone's throw from the sprawling Weetwood police station. It had rained constantly and poor Pete Watson, stopwatch in hand and his hood pulled up tight against the summer downpour, had watched and encouraged and timed a handful of club members as they ran laps, half-laps, three-quarter laps, two-lap warm-downs, fast sprints and easy recoveries. Everyone was exhausted and wanting to get home, but Gary seemed keen to host a small invite-only meeting of some sort in the tap room of an uninviting student pub. Gary came in last, bleached hair untouched since that one final 59 second 440-yard run. He greeted the three, saw that they already had drinks, complained that nobody had got him one, and sauntered to the bar to order a pint of cider.

Joke:

A punk walks into a bar. Before he has a chance to order a drink, a tiny voice says, "I like your tattoos. And the bleached hair is pretty cool."

The punk looks around and sees nobody, so he says to the bartender, "Who said that?"

The bartender says, "Oh don't worry. That's just the complimentary peanuts."

The punk buys a pint of cider and as he's about to leave the bar a different voice says, "Your hair's a bloody mess! And those ripped jeans stink."

The punk looks around and again sees nobody.

"Who was *that*?"

The bartender finishes cleaning a glass. "Don't worry about it. It's just the cigarette machine – it's out of order."

Gary sat down and the other three waited as he had a first drink of his pint.

"Right. I got a phone call. Off Danny Hughes."

He paused as if to give someone space to ask what Danny had said, but no-one said a word. The rain sprayed against the pub's windows and the jukebox played a song about turtles from the soundtrack of the new *Mutant Ninja Turtles* film. It was number one. Truly, punk had come and gone and died a thousand deaths.

"Anyway, Danny says he's sending a team from England to the

European Team Relay Championships in Italy. And it's a Pudsey & Bramley team, since we won the British and English."

The table erupted in a mixture of exclamation and relief, excited talk and questions.

"But, thing is, erm, not to put a dampener on it or anything, but we can only take three. It's a three-man relay. And obviously I asked you three because, well, there's me, and then there's you three all about equal."

The gravity of what Gary was explaining was beginning to dawn on the athletes around the table. The chit and the chat disappeared along with the smiles. All three agreed with Gary that they were running equally well – throughout the season they'd been scrapping and battling up and down all sorts of races, short and steep, long and undulating, straight-up-and-back-down, four-hour multiple peak slogs, and their positions had constantly switched. And besides which, no-one was prepared to admit they were weaker or slower than the other two.

"So I mean, basically it means one of you can't go, so, well, we have to work out who that will be. Unless one of you can't make it, which will make this easier."

He pulled out a folded scrap of paper from his inside jacket pocket, opened it and read out loud what scant details he had from Danny, including dates and times. The three runners didn't even pull their diaries out – they all declared immediately that they were able to go. Why wouldn't they? An all-expenses-paid trip to Italy to represent your country? Do bears run in the woods? Does the Pope run in a big hat?

"Right then. That's a problem."

Another pause. They all took a swig of their drinks. Richard Pallister, one of the three, smiled. "I know what's coming."

"You do?"

"Yeah. Beer mats."

Another pause. Gary clasped his hands tighter around his glass.

"I think it'll have to be, won't it?"

Beermats had a special place in Pudsey & Bramley mythology. Over the years, when members of other clubs had spent too long in the post-race pub with whichever bunch of P&B stragglers were in there, when those members of other clubs had become separated from their club mates, when they were encircled at a table, distanced from their herd and tipsily, smilingly vulnerable – someone would tear the design from the face of a beermat and, on the revealed off-white card, biro a contract:

I, ..., AGREE TO JOIN PUDSEY & BRAMLEY ATHLETICS CLUB, AND WILL FROM THIS DAY FORWARD WEAR THE CLARET AND GOLD WITH PRIDE. SIGNED,

....

Once signed, the contract/beermat was obviously legally binding. Beermats had another role to play, though.

You could tear one up into three equally-sized pieces, scrawl a felt-tip pen 'X' on one of the pieces, fold and twist them and place them in an ashtray. 'X' loses. The Black Spot. The Ace of Spades. The Tarot's Grim Reaper. You get the 'X', you stay at home while the others get an England vest and a free trip to Italy.

And this is what they did. They picked a team to represent England in an international race by drawing bits of beermat from an ashtray. And the loser? The loser stayed at home and wrote a book about it.

IMRF – International Mountain Running Federation
ICMR – International Committee of Mountain Running
FRA – Fell Runners Association
AAA – Amateur Athletics Association
IAAF – International Association of Athletics Federations
IFCA – International Federation of Confusing Acronyms

CHAPTER 11

"In fact, punk rock means – exemplary manners to your fellow human beings."
— *Joe Strummer*

The headline on the front of the *Leeds Student* newspaper was simply, in four-inch-high letters, 'RIOT'. The text below explained:

'Thirty-four arrests at ALF gig. Leeds University Union witnessed a full blown riot on Monday night as over 150 Animal Liberation Front Supporters clashed with police in the most violent scenes ever seen in the history of the Union.'

The Riley-Smith Hall, a large red-brick cube normally reserved for freshers' week balls, exams, recruitment expos and performances by the University's various theatre societies, jutted out from the Union foyer, its polished wooden floor and low stage emptied of chairs and tables. It was mid-afternoon and the PA was being wheeled in through a back entrance, huge stacks of speakers balanced on two-wheeled trolleys. Some of the bands had already arrived and were sitting around the hall eating canteen sandwiches and swigging from cans of cheap lager. They'd come from all over the country to play – City Indians from Derby, Oi Polloi from Edinburgh, anarcho-squatters Chumbawamba from just up the road in Armley and headliners Conflict from London.

The gig was billed – on flyers and stickers that had been flooding the Yorkshire area squat scene for months – as a benefit for the Leeds Bust Fund, rather than the ALF Bust Fund as *Leeds Student* suggested. The Leeds Bust Fund had been set up by various clumps of anarchists and squatters in Leeds to help pay off the fines of people arrested in the Leeds area during various direct actions. Getting arrested had become almost an unavoidable part of the squatting and alternative lifestyle; the mid-1980s had seen an upsurge in locally grown actions, demonstrations and protests which had been radicalised and fomented by Margaret Thatcher's brand of individualist Conservatism and by Crass's brand of individualist punk rock. Thatcher's claim that "there is no such thing as society" echoed the Sex Pistols' earlier cries of 'No Fuuuuutuuuuure!' and the whole mixed-up ball of conflicting messages added up to a generation of disenfranchised and disregarded teenagers. The fall-out from the Tories' year-long battle to crush the miners could be measured in the length of queues at the job centres and the increasing gap between rich and poor.

The anti-nuclear and animal rights single-issue politics of the early 1980s gave way to a much more broad-based anarchism encompassing squatters, anti-fascist groups, animal liberation activists, strike support groups and anyone who felt motivated to resist the daily encroachment of the Conservative government's increasingly policed state. Very often the same people would be involved in all of the above actions: on the streets rattling collection tins for the miners by day, raiding a factory farm by night. Getting arrested was a badge you could wear with pride, alongside all the neatly-stencilled slogans on your T-shirts.

As the PA inside the Riley-Smith Hall was assembled and bands began to plug in amps and tune up guitars, as gaggles of punks from all over the north of England began to wander into the Union buildings to the thud thud thud thud thud thud thud thud thud thud of a bass drum being soundchecked, as students began to warily eye the growing numbers of black-clad kids drinking from two-litre bottles of cider, as the gig's organisers began to negotiate with the hired university security (actually members of the Uni rugby society, big lads with red cheeks and cropped curly hair and sensible shoes), as all this noise was gathering and building, and specifically as one hilariously drunk lad in a studded leather jacket, biker boots and tartan trousers picked up an abandoned chair he found by the Riley-Smith Hall's entrance and swung it against the glass panel of the door, smashing it, shocked, wondering what he'd done, being jumped on by three of the rugby club bouncers and hauled off to be held in the porter's office until the police arrived and marched him off to the bridewell in the centre of Leeds, as all these signs and omens and portents were rising to the surface of the afternoon – yes, still only the afternoon – it started to become clear that there was a developing irony in the idea of a gig raising money for people who had arrest charges, court cases and fines looking very much like it would end up in people having arrest charges, court cases and fines. Build up the Bust Fund, we're gonna need it.

The doors opened at 7pm and the hall filled to bursting with several hundred of these waifs and strays, clowns and freaks, misshapes and mutants, crackpots and weirdos, mavericks and oddballs. The bands began to play, short sharp sets, half an hour each of ear-bashing noise, all flailing drumsticks and barre chords and yelled vocals. They sang of peace and it sounded like war. One of the bands stopped, slowed down, played a song with a tune, with a chorus, with a harmony, and a girl in the audience wearing white face-paint and dark, dark eye make-up, threw an empty bottle of Newcastle Brown Ale at them. They played on and she threw another. Someone in the audience shouted at her, screamed, gestured, and got punched in the face. Another band came and played, and somewhere at the back of the hall a fight broke out – a pinched-face punk wearing trousers that had been inexpertly fashioned from beer towels pulled a knife out, started waving it around, and tension in the room rose above the level of the band's racket.

Gary watched the carnival going on around him, nonplussed at the madhouse of black denim and noise. Over by the hall's huge windows he could see someone he'd been keeping an eye on, an overweight bloke in a black leather jacket. Gary had seen him a few times before, either at Adam & Eve's or at Bradford's 1 in 12 Club; he was one of the Huddersfield contingent that travelled on the train to punk gigs around West Yorkshire. Two weeks before the Riley-Smith Hall concert, Gary had seen him at a Varukers gig, wearing the same leather jacket; he had stood out because, painted in bold white letters on the back of the tatty jacket, had been the slogan:

MEAT MEANS YUM YUM
VEGGIE SCUM

…which was like a red rag to the bullish veggie punks for whom 'meat means murder' was a clarion call. Tonight's headliners Conflict, a gang of working-class lads who'd taken the Crass template and used it to create something more aggressive and more extreme, had written a song called 'Meat Means Murder':

The factory is churning out all processed packed and neat
An obscure butchered substance and the label reads Meat
Hidden behind false names such as Pork, Ham, Veal, and Beef
An eye's an eye, a life's a life, the now forgotten belief
And every day production lines are feeding out this farce
To end up on a table then shot out of an arse

Conflict rejected the pacifist ideology of their predecessors Crass and Discharge, adopting instead some street-level brute force to back up their arguments. Having watched bands like Crass, Sham 69 and Angelic Upstarts being crippled and demoralised by countless stage invasions by right-wing skinheads, Conflict would turn up at concerts with a handful of their mates and a bag of baseball bats.

Gary decided he ought to confront Mr Yum Yum, and with two large bottles of Merrydown cider already scrapping with each other somewhere between his stomach and his brain, he sauntered across to 'have words'. Except that, as he found out when he checked out the back of Yum Yum's jacket, the offending Yum Yums had been erased and replaced with the single word 'Conflict'. It was beautifully painted, Gary had to concede – an old English font with decorative scrolls spiralling out from the 'f' and the 't' – but that was beside the point. If anything, this was even worse than 'Yum Yum Veggie Scum'; it was dishonest and cowardly. He shouted above the rhythmic noise of Oi Polloi, a repetitive cycle of the same three chords going round and round and round and round.

"Hey, what's that?"

"What's what?"

"That, on your back. Last time I saw you it said 'Yum Yum Veggie Scum', and you've changed it 'cos you're at a Conflict gig."

"Yeah, so?"

"So that makes you a wanker."

"You what?"

"I said that makes you a wanker."

The two squared up. It had only been a couple of months since Gary had been accidentally punched in the face by a flailing dancer at an Anti-System concert in Bradford; he'd won the Simon's Seat race shortly afterwards sporting a comical shiner and looking for all the world like he'd been in a fistfight. Yum Yum grew a couple of inches taller.

"If I'm a wanker what are you?"

Gary noticed now that Yum Yum had friends with him, and they were circling, moving in, clenching their fists. The hall suddenly felt hotter, louder and darker, the walls closed in, the edges of Gary's vision blurring and smudging. Gary knew he couldn't back down, and tightened his arm, quickly counting down to point zero, here we go, hold your breath, ready now –

Someone shouted above the noise, "Cops!" And everyone turned to look. At the back of the hall the swing doors flew open and punks began to move quickly towards the exit and out into the main Union foyer. The band stopped playing as the audience ran, shouted, pushed and pulled. Yum Yum disappeared as Gary scanned the room for his mates. Gone, gone with the heaving mass of the crowd, out of sight and towards whatever was happening outside. Gary moved with the coagulated lump of bodies, rushing to the door, down the wide steps and across the foyer, through the double doors and out into the evening, warm and dense with moving people, a mobocracy, pandemonium and turmoil, and across the small square a line of police forming and doubling and doubling again as dark blue vans screeched to a halt and disgorged uniformed officers, most of them with truncheons already drawn.

"What's going on?!" shouted Gary to nobody and everybody at the same time. A girl with pink and blue hair shouted back.

"Cops have started arresting anyone trying to leave the square. Anyone who looks like they're from the concert."

"What for?"

"Security called them, they couldn't stop the fighting. There's a lad from the gig they got in the porter's office, they beat him up, someone said he had to go to the hospital to have stitches, he was one of the Bradford punks, they only –" she stopped mid-sentence.

"Look!"

She pointed up the street, towards the corner where Lifton Place met Cromer Terrace, overlooked by huge Victorian stone buildings with their great bay windows and massive slabs of front doors, houses where ancient academics would sit in leather studded armchairs and discuss poetry with timid first years in front of well-kept open fires. More police vans were arriving, one after each other, three, four, five, all emptying out their load of cops who marched straight up the university precinct to join the lines of officers standing firmly and defiantly across from the union's main entrance.

Gary took out his last remaining bottle of cider from the inside pocket of his jacket and started to swig. He offered the girl a drink; she took it, had a mouthful and passed it back. The mood of the steadily-building crowd was changing now. The adrenalin rush of the stampede was settling into a sense of communal anger, a bolshy, cocky rage. There was also a spreading feeling of euphoria, the buzz of expectation. Nobody was moving back into the hall; the gig had effectively transported itself into the courtyard, the entertainment out here was going to be something else entirely.

A punk balancing on the low railings outside the hall threw a half-full can of lager at the police line and a cheer went up. The line dodged and shifted but retracted immediately, perfectly. Another can sailed over, falling short, then a bottle. It smashed at the feet of the first line of police and at this, the lines moved forward, a step at a time, now three or four deep with more joining their ranks as they moved down into the courtyard. A kid who couldn't have been older than 14 made a run for the steps leading off to the right towards the grand and looming Parkinson Building, but just when the crowd thought he was going to evade the front line of police he was caught by the shoulder and brought to the ground, where three or four cops grabbed him, pulling him legs-first back through their lines, kicking and punching as they went. At this, the crowd surged forward and a hail of missiles flew across the square – the noise rose to a crescendo, all shouts and cries and howls and whoops and screams. Things were happening everywhere, pockets of action sparking and dying and reappearing, flurries and fluster and fuss.

Gary decided to try to escape the madness. The door behind him was now shut from the inside and the only way out was through the police lines. He made a run for it, dodging in and out of the scraps and brawls, up to his left, through the first few groups of police who were busy thrashing away with their batons and dragging punks out of the yard and towards the waiting vans. He reached the first in the line of vans and, dodging around it, was felled, bang, by a heavy blow that caught him on the shoulder, spun him around and threw him to the floor. The driver of the van had waited until Gary had drawn level with his window and opened the door straight into him, smashing his arm. The policeman jumped on him and was quickly joined by two other officers who manhandled Gary away from the van and towards one of the house's neat front gardens, where they threw him straight into the hedge, losing their grip on him for a second. He instinctively scrambled upright and lashed out with his feet, catching one of the officers, then began to run, off up the street, chased now by all three cops. They couldn't catch him; of course they couldn't. He was a runner. He trained twice a day. He'd run for England. He could run up and down mountains. A police car appeared from nowhere to his left, turning out of a side street and catching up with him. He was a runner. He trained twice a day. He'd run for England. He could run up and down mountains. He couldn't outrun a car.

He was cornered halfway up the street, the police vehicle screaming to a halt in front of him right across the pavement, the passenger-side cop leaping out to cut off any possible escape. Within a few seconds he had five police officers on top of him, jabbing and kicking and pushing their gloved fists into his back. They dragged him back down the road and threw him into the back of a Transit van, slamming the doors shut behind him. Inside the van were four others who'd been bundled in there, swearing and gasping and shouting. Outside, the chaos continued for what seemed like ages but was a matter of ten, fifteen minutes. Then it went quiet, and quieter still, until all that could be heard from the inside of the van were the shouts of commanding officers barking instructions. Finally a driver and his mate jumped into the front, breathing heavily, separated from the back by a reinforced grill. The driver shouted toward the back –

"Right then ladies! Let's get you to the station."

A dozen of those arrested were dragged, pushed and slapped along the long tiled corridor that ran underneath the Town Hall, the infamous Leeds Bridewell, its green-and-cream Victorian functionality broken at intervals by huge and heavy doors, iron and studded with ancient bolts, each one with a six-inch square metal slider covering a food hatch. They were lined up in the holding station, bruised, muttering, tired. The cops who'd thrown Gary into the hedge – including the one he'd lashed out at and kicked – were brought in to get their stories straight, identify who'd done what, compare notes. They walked down the line, three of them, collars unbuttoned and ties loosened, breathing in the adrenalin and sensing their power. One young officer stopped in front of Gary and looked him in the eye. Five, ten, fifteen seconds. Then he carried on, stopped, snorted, and stuck his finger in the chest of a bigger lad, a Scottish punk with bleached hair who'd travelled down from Paisley for the concert, saying,

"This is the cunt. Kicked me when I was on the floor."

"No I didn't."

"Yes you did. If I say you did, you did."

Gary kept quiet as the bigger lad was pulled out of the line and led off down the corridor. The procession moved on.

The following morning Gary was charged with affray and a month later, on a drizzly Thursday afternoon, he pleaded guilty at Leeds Crown Court in front of a judge who had been given the job of throwing whatever book he could find at the thirty-four punks arrested that night. Gary took his running kit with him in a rucksack, and after being ticked off by the judge and fined £180 plus 180 hours community service – to be spent working at the local RSPCA in Burley – he got changed in the Crown Court toilets and ran home, taking the roundabout route out along the Leeds-Liverpool canal and through the parks and ginnels. He had some races to get in training for.

CHAPTER 12

"I believe that all wisdom consists in caring immensely for a few right things, and not caring a straw about the rest."
— John Buchan

In the late summer of 1987, Leeds's Chapeltown district was hit by riots after police had arrested and beaten up a 17-year-old black boy. Cars and shops were attacked, burned and bombed as the riot spread across the area. A sex shop on the main Chapeltown Road – for over a year the focus of local community protests – was burned to the ground, not least because of the discovery that the police were using its upstairs flat as a base for their surveillance of drug-dealing in the area. The riot lasted for three days, the fires seen right across Leeds.

Meanwhile, 300 miles north of the riots, Leeds's very own veteran DJ and television presenter Jimmy Savile was enjoying his role as honorary Chieftain at the Fort William showground where, with Ben Nevis as a backdrop, a band of Scottish pipers in traditional dress led a parade around the field to signal the start of the town's annual Highland Games. Children ran to the ice cream stands, huge men in heavy boots and kilts tossed cabers and threw hammers, and an indistinct loudspeaker soundtracked the mock swordfights. Savile, complete with a tartan tracksuit, pink sunglasses and trademark cigar, had long been the regular ceremonial face of the Games and owned a 200-year-old cottage up the road in Glencoe. The beer tent was doing good business, traditional Scottish dancers danced traditional Scottish dances, red-and-yellow flags flew above the showground's 400-metre grass track, and a large crowd was gathering to see the finish of the Half Ben Nevis race, the second race in three days of the 'Triple Hirple', Lochaber AC's trio of fell races based around the Fort William games. The previous day's Meall-an-T race was a 3-mile race that scrambled up and down rough track and heather; today the route led out along Glen Nevis and climbed up steeply to the old Nevis path before turning at the Red Burn, a distance of just under six miles with a record that had belonged to Colin Donnelly since 1983. Nobody had won all three races.

Jimmy Savile was entertaining the crowds at the finish as Gary entered the park to cheers and applause. Jimmy never liked being upstaged, and the arrival of a young lad at the head of the race, a lad with a shock of dyed-pink hair, unnerved him. Gary crossed the finish line as he did in the previous day's race, in first place, breathless but smiling. An hour later, showered and changed and at the prize-giving, Gary stood, embarrassed, next to the booming caricature in the tartan tracksuit. Jimmy leaned over and in to Gary, telling him and anyone within earshot that he needed to "have a word".

"Now then sir. They tell me you're from Leeds?"

"Aye."

"Put it there son," he grinned, holding out his hand. They shook. Savile held onto the half-smoked cigar in his other hand, a prop, part of his clown outfit. He carried on talking, that's what he'd always done, that was his job, his trademark, the non-stop gabbing and joshing and blather and prattle and gibberish and drivel, the half-yodelled laughter and the inconsequential, meaningless catchphrases. As it happens, guys and gals, now then now then, goodness gracious.

"Twenty years younger and I'd have raced up there with you. Probably beat you an' all!"

Gary grinned awkwardly.

"And what's with this pink then? You trying to upstage me? That won't do, no it won't, won't do at all."

Gary grinned awkwardly.

"Look at mine – Go Faster Hair I call it. Yours must be Go Even Faster hair."

Gary grinned awkwardly.

Savile lowered his voice and put an arm around Gary's shoulder, drawing him away from the gathering onlookers.

"Seriously, though. What's your name again?"

"Gary."

"Gary. Listen Gary, seriously though. This is a goldmine."

He pointed first at his own hair and then at Gary's. Then he motioned down to Gary's Amebix T-Shirt and ripped black jeans, more rips than jeans, his leather studded belt hung low, his boots sloppy and unfastened.

"A goldmine. Take my advice, stay weird. People love weird. You can market weird. Look at me. Injured in a mining accident, down the pits at South Kirkby, 14-year-old, who wants a crippled ex-miner? Tell you what though, that bang on the head down the mine, it shook some nonsense into me. And I discovered that people love nonsense. It's all nonsense, isn't it? Fun and nonsense."

Gary was getting bored now. This was turning into the kind of comic monologue Gary had watched on old black-and-white TV comedy shows, ageing comedians with their tired repetition and needy egos. For a split second, Gary saw himself in thirty, forty, fifty years' time, pink-haired and in a UK Subs shirt, clowning around in a Pudsey & Bramley-coloured tracksuit.

"Take my advice, son – what was the name again?"

"Gary."

"Gary, right. Take my advice, ditch the running, keep up the nonsense. Make a fortune, you will."

With that he wheeled around to sign autographs and have his picture taken, arms outstretched in a gesture of 'who wants me', the honorary Highland Chieftain with his bang on the head and his words of wisdom and his cigar. Clunk click, every trip.

Later that day the organisers of the Games, sitting at a long wooden trestle table in the showfield's HQ tent, met to discuss whether they could take any disciplinary action against the day's fell race winner for immediately selling his winning vouchers – to be redeemed at local stores – for cash.

*

Pudsey & Bramley Athletics Club officially met on a Tuesday night at Priesthorpe School on the ring road between Leeds and Bradford. Unofficially the team's hardcore group of fell runners met on Mondays at the old cinder 440-yard track out at Lawnswood and on Wednesdays up at Otley Chevin. The Weetwood cinder track belonged to Leeds University but had been left unused for several years as the student athletes trained across at the Leeds Beckett site on the new tartan track; floodlit, secure and with a two-storey clubhouse. Pudsey's Pete Watson – a legend at the club for his seven victories in the Burnsall Fell Race in the 1960s – turned up on Mondays and, like the rest of the club members, ducked under the locked gates with his notepad, pen and stopwatch. Pete was short and stocky, he didn't look like a fell runner; but then, what did fell runners look like? They came in most shapes and sizes, different horses for different courses, they were built not just to run but to climb, to clamber, to leap, to slide, to spring, to tumble – in torrential rain, baking heat, through mud, over loose rock, down scree slopes, up riverbeds. The runners who turned up on a Monday to run measured distances around the Weetwood track fitted the description 'fell runner' if only because they were a disparate assortment of athletes who barely suited the description 'athlete'. Some, like Richard Pallister and the brothers Brian and Paul Stevenson, had been around the club for a while. Non-stop chatterbox Ady Illingworth, and tall, bespectacled Mike Falgate were near-neighbours in Pudsey, round a few corners from printer Alan Greenwood and a hop, skip and jump from madly grinning Paul Gaines. Paul was an organiser, a do-er, a let's-get-it-sorted type; he, like the rest, realised that there was now a chemistry in the club that centred around Gary Devine but spun out to a growing number of runners who could, and would, somehow perform well above their potential for this club. Some Pudsey runners were spread across West Leeds and beyond. Jack Maitland would periodically return from his round-the-world jaunts to run in the club's colours, some like Graham Kirkbright had gravitated toward the club as it started to get a reputation as a strong and successful fell running club. From 'hear him before you see him' Jamie Smith to 'didn't notice you were here' Danbert Nobacon (you'd never believe he was the exhibitionist lead singer in a band, as well as an advocate of public nudity and cross-dressing), this disparate and disorganised bunch began to buy into the idea of a club that punched above its weight, that could compete against the best, basing their rapid improvement on an unspoken formula of nihilism and fun – distancing themselves from athleticism's off-the-peg mantras and cliches:

No pain, no gain.
Second is nowhere.
If it's easy, you're doing it wrong.
If you fail to prepare, prepare to fail.
Hard work beats talent when talent doesn't work hard.
Good is no good when better is expected.
Persistence changes failure into achievement.
Your worst enemy lives between your ears.
The difference between impossible and possible is determination.
You've gotta believe it to achieve it.

Nihilism is the belief that the moral and religious principles underpinning the way society acts are meaningless. It questions the grounds on which Western culture has based its truths; in the hands of the punk generation it meant, 'Question authority. Question everything.' In the words of Johnny Rotten:

We're so pretty, oh so pretty –
Vacant
And we don't care
(Sex Pistols 'Pretty Vacant')

And on the other hand, there was fun. Treating the sport as play, as recreation, climbing hills for enjoyment, for a blast. Celebrating the absurdity of racing up and down mountains, freewheeling in the joy of it all. And these adventures, having them together with your friends, turning an athletics club into a social club. Gary had run for three different clubs now, and each one had understood his potential. His two previous clubs offered him training, coaching, advice, a strong team ethic, the chance to be part of a winning club. Gary wanted that, but more – what he got at Pudsey & Bramley was a bunch of athletic misfits who wanted to have fun, and whose version of running somehow matched his version of punk. Of course they wanted to win. They wanted to be the best runners in every race they turned up at. But having turned up, they wanted to enjoy themselves. As a club, and as a team. One of Gary's problems as a runner, which he readily admitted, was that he jeopardised his chances of excelling at international level by racing far too much during the season – but he couldn't stop, because he loved to race. And his favourite races, the races he looked forward to most, were the team relays; where he ran not for himself but as part of Pudsey & Bramley AC.

Picture the Bash Street Kids in maroon and gold vests. The Bash Street Kids, exploding beyond the confines of *The Beano* every week, had been created by avowed anarchist and cartoonist Leo Baxendale to poke fun at authority, and to do it in the guise of a dysfunctional gang of school kids at war with their strict teacher. Danny (Gary) in his skull-and-crossbones jumper and red cap, creating pranks and leading the gang, 'Erbert (Willie Gaunt) the short-sighted sidekick who inadvertently wreaks havoc, Plug (Ady Illingworth), gangling and lanky, a comic and an entertainer, Sidney (Jamie Smith) a loud-mouthed trickster who gets into fights with the others, Wilfrid (Danbert Nobacon) quiet and shy until called upon to create mischief, and on and on and on and bursting out of the school yard chased by Teacher, heading for the hills and not coming back.

At the Weetwood track, Pete Watson turned the track sessions into competitive games, and the competition between the club's runners began to sharpen everyone up. Never mind that Pete's little scraps of paper which biro'd every runner's split times and were dutifully given out at the end of each session inevitably ended up in the wash, in the bin or in the bottom of bottomless kitbags. Wednesday evening's hill-training sessions over on Otley Chevin weren't run against stopwatches but against every team-mate. Gary refused to allow anyone to beat him on these five- or six-minute lung-bursting climbs, though everyone tried. Younger club members like Colin Walker, already excelling at schools cross-country, treated the Wednesday hill reps as though they were races – and significantly upped the overall quality of the rest of the team. And through it all there was the laughing and the mickey-taking and the encouraging and the planning, usually only two or three weeks ahead: which races were coming up, who was driving, has anyone done that one before, which other teams are turning up, which shoes are best to run in, is there a pub for after the race.

Most of this stuff wouldn't be vastly different at any other fell running club – the sport encouraged a culture of fun and camaraderie, a love of the hills and a joy in competing. Fell running's history was peppered with stories of wayward athletes breaking rules and protocols, upsetting the authorities, embarrassing pub arguments and post-race drinkers stripping naked and running down high streets. But rarely has a club so readily adopted an ethos and philosophy that sprang from such an *unathletic* source as punk; and never had a club made this a basis for winning things. Essentially, the combined attitudes of 'we don't care' and 'let's make it fun' somehow became a successful formula.

'I don't care' comes in two varieties. There's the 'I don't care' that stops you trying, that is a shortcut to laziness, that means can't be bothered, can't be arsed, don't give a shit, meh, whatever, shrugs shoulders, turns away and pulls the covers up tighter and falls back asleep. And then there's the 'I don't care' that is defiant, insolent, I'll-do-it-in-spite-of-you, cavalier and brazen and snotty – in the words of punk band Crass, a big 'So What?'

Well they say they're going to send me away
Say they're going to make me pay
We're sorry but you've got to go
You were naughty, you said 'no' –
So what?
So what?
So what?

Fell running allows that 'so what' into sport, it's got a belligerence and cockiness that just isn't in most other sports. There's the story of the top-class Bingley Harriers runner, used to racing on a track or in flat cross-country races that all too often consist of laps of playing fields, who travelled to Scotland to compete in the Ben Nevis race. Being an elite athlete he made it to the summit of the mountain inside the top five runners, a brilliant achievement. On turning at the top he came to where the loose and rocky path zig-zagged its way up the top third of the Ben and was horrified to see that all the fell runners around him ignored the path that they'd run up and instead cut straight across the zigs and the zags, hurtling recklessly down the boulder-fields. He stopped dead, muttered "No way!" And descended carefully by the path. He finished somewhere around the top 100 or so. Fell running gives you the chance to say 'I don't care' when told that it's too steep, too rocky, too wet, too long, too treacherous, too slippy, too dangerous, too cold, too hot, too dicey, too muddy, too icy, too risky.

By the time Gary hit his 21st birthday he was still trying to find a balance between the extremes of athletic excellence and punk rock nihilism, attempting to discover an equilibrium, a good place. He had two distinct social groups around him, and each knew next-to-nothing about the other, so it was always strangely funny when the two happened to bump into one another, when one lot got a glimpse of what was happening on the other side. Every year Gary had a planned sabbatical from running, usually around Christmas and New Year. He'd still go out for training runs, but he wouldn't race for several weeks – the early-December Calderdale Way Relay, where he was usually partnered with Jack Maitland, would be his last race until mid-January. The idea was to give himself some breathing space, to halt the week-in, week-out pattern that top-level running thrives on; with his Pudsey & Bramley team-mates there was almost always a race to get to on a Saturday, which often meant travelling on Friday and returning on Sunday, wild camping (farmers' fields, football pitches, grassy ring-road roundabouts), drinking, racing, recovering and generally filling up all the weekend's available space. The annual break was a time to tip the balance away from the races and the hill reps and the track sessions and over-indulge instead in the chaotic, drunken waywardness of punk – letting off steam to the sound of Napalm Death, now punk's self-declared fastest, loudest band. It had been a tough year and the move from junior to senior racing had taken a fair amount out of Gary, and maintaining the awkward balance between punk rock and fell running wasn't always easy.

Gary's last race of 1987 was the classic, tough Winter Hill race in Lancashire, and like a lot of races, the hill had its own peculiar history. In the summer of 1896, Colonel Richard Henry Ainsworth, an aristocratic type residing in a mansion on the outskirts of Bolton, decided to cut off public access to the wide open moorland of Winter Hill. As the hill's coal stocks had dwindled he realised he could make revenue from opening the moor to grouse-shooting. He erected gates across access roads, fixed them with 'Trespassers Will Be Prosecuted' signs and hired men to stand guard and warn people off the property. The public outcry led to a small advertisement appearing in the local Bolton paper, inviting the public to join a demonstration on an upcoming September Sunday morning, to test the right of way over Winter Hill.

A crowd of 1000 met in Bolton to listen to some speeches. Numbers increased tenfold as they marched up Halliwell Road towards the edge of the moor, where they were confronted by a small contingent of police. According to the *Bolton Chronicle*, 'Amid the lusty shouting of the crowd the gate was attacked by powerful hands… short work was made of the barrier, and with a ring of triumph the demonstrators rushed through onto the disputed territory.' Plans were soon in place to repeat the procession. A song was commissioned.

Will yo' come o' Sunday morning
For a walk o'er Winter Hill
Ten thousand went last Sunday
But there's room for thousands still!
Oh the moors are rare and bonny
And the heather's sweet and fine
And the road across this hill top
Is the public's – yours and mine!

Not quite the Sex Pistols, but the spirit was similar… Despite some rain the following Sunday, 10,000 people again set off for Winter Hill, and though sixty police officers were dispatched to guard the path to the moor, once again the gates were broken and access gained. Ainsworth resorted to the courts, but despite winning some £600 in compensation, the public's sense of both anger and power had been kindled.

A fair amount of the land that is used for fell racing has a history of access and ownership disputes, and races run over formerly private land come with a sense of freedom and commonality. These hills have become our playground through the efforts of history's firebrands and objectors, the dissenters who were prepared to protest to gain public rights of way across the mountaintops and valley bottoms. The Winter Hill race, a tough 11-mile course that repeatedly drops to the hill's skirt before climbing its flanks, was a classic late-season bog-trot, notorious for the peat groughs which could grab runners by the feet and suck them in and down, down, down into the slurping, bubbling, brown mass. Paths across some of the routes were few and far between, with route choice, stamina and an ability to swim being essential. That this unwelcoming quagmire was the site of a historic battle for access reinforces the idea that our land – in all its various forms – is a shared playground.

At face value this wasn't Gary's type of race. Having secured first place in the year's Intermediate English Championship, he might have eased off into late autumn, but instead Gary opted to keep racing up until winter really set in. The back part of the year was stormy; but while Winter Hill in late November was infamously cold and often saw the first snow of the season, this year the race would be run under clear skies and with a hard frost covering the worst of the bog. Still bloody cold, though. The race favourites were the sport's hard men, those runners who loved the long, tough courses, Colin Valentine, Graham Schofield and former winner and England international Ray Owen. The question before the race was, as Gary joked to his team-mates, how many pairs of underpants to wear. On the first long descent, careering in and out of a light covering of fresh snow, Gary and Ray Owen pulled away from the rest of the field, and the race became an attritional head-to-head between the two. Not knowing the course, Gary stayed behind Ray, step for step over the stiles and across the bogs, until the final mile. As the race climbed one last time underneath Rivington Pike, up the drag of Roynton Road before the descent to the finish, Gary made his move and pulled clear, winning by just eight seconds.

On the way home from the race, driving alone for a change, he had space and time to think about the season and about his performance on the day. It wasn't anywhere near the most competitive field he'd competed in, but he felt that it was a significant win for him – it gave him confidence that he could battle it out in heavy conditions, he wasn't scared of the different kinds of races and weathers, and above all it proved that he was getting stronger. He put in an Antisect cassette tape and turned up the volume, travelling along the M62 nodding his head in time with the music and passing from one world to another.

*

Gary had moved into the ground-floor room of a shared house on Victoria Road with his girlfriend Zombie, his dog Sheba and a small (but growing) collection of cups and shields from various races. The ever-present kitbag, the most permanent and loyal fixture in Gary's nomadic lifestyle, sat centre stage as always, open and overflowing. He still had the cheek to take a bundle of clothes (running stuff, not everyday stuff. That rarely got washed) round to his mum's house every couple of weeks in one of those huge multicoloured striped bags with handles that always break and with zips that never work; it was his way of keeping in touch with his family. He'd either stay around his mum's house and sit with his younger sister watching whatever happened to be on the TV while his mucky vests and shorts were whizzing around in a noisy machine in the kitchen – *Grange*

Hill, *Spitting Image*, *Antiques Roadshow*, *Only Fools and Horses*, *Blackadder*, *This Is Your Life* – or he'd disappear and promise to come round the following day to pick up his cleaned, ironed and folded washing. His dad Hughie still went to races when he could, even venturing abroad when he gave himself time off work, driving to the continent in his builders van with a collection of fell runners in the back, hitting whichever local bar was closest to the finish line.

Gary now didn't have a TV in his room – he rarely had time to sit and watch anything (and there was nothing to sit on). Through the year, life was split between training, going to gigs and parties, racing, and labouring for his dad, so when the winter break came around it was a welcome break in the everyday ordinariness of punk rock mountain running. Three shopping days to Christmas and there was a sheepish knock on the door. Sheepish in its lightness, its "I'm not sure if this is the right house" caution. Sheba barked loudly and Gary told her "Shhh!" He was preparing her food, the can was open and he already had a fork stabbed into its prime jellied contents, but now he stopped and turned to the door. Sheba barked again.

"Shut it!"

She ignored him and barked loudly again, and again, and again, and again.

"Sit!"

And again and again.

Gary left his room with the full tin of dog food in his hand, a fork sticking out, driving Sheba crazy. The barks turned into whimpers as he disappeared down the corridor to the front door, past the bike with the puncture that was a permanent obstacle along with a heap of plastic piping that was what remained of an attempt to fix the bathroom plumbing. He opened the door and there stood the Stevenson brothers, Paul and Brian. It was strange seeing them in their civvies, in T-shirts and jeans and sensible shoes, and not in their tracksuits and running shoes and maroon 'n' yellow vests. The last time Gary had seen Stevie was at an Indian restaurant called The Shama on the way back from the Langdale Pike race in the Lake District. The team were crammed into three cars and the plan was to stop on the way back to Yorkshire, somewhere along the A65, for a drink and something to eat, but as soon as they'd walked into The Courtyard pub – or rather, as it styled itself, 'Brasserie at The Courtyard' – the owner had rushed from behind the bar to breathlessly let the team know that they wouldn't be served, because (indicate preference) –

a) Sorry we don't cater for groups
b) Sorry our chef is ill
c) Sorry all our tables are booked
d) Sorry we're expecting a wedding party
e) Sorry we're closing early this evening
f) Sorry the bar manager's wife is having a baby
   and he's had to leave early

– and so with muttered swearing that carried delicately over the room's embarrassed tinkle of knives and forks, the whole team turned tail and decided on a curry in Shipley instead. The Shama welcomed everyone and dragged together a huge collection of tables to make one banquet-sized buffet groaning with massively over-ordered plates of masala, biryani, tikka, chapatti, dal, korma, paratha, jalfrezi, tandoori, aloo and paneer. By the time it had all arrived, Stevie was shattered from two pints of Kingfisher and a 14-mile race around the Langdale Pikes that climbed around 4,000 feet and took in Bowfell, the Crinkle Crags and Pike o' Blisco, and instead of tucking into his food, and despite the loud chatter machine-gunning its patterns across the table, he put his head gently onto his plate of warm chapatti and fell asleep. Ady had suggested they all quietly leave at the end of the meal, leaving him to wake up to an empty table and half a chapatti stuck to his face, but his brother Brian instead slapped him awake so he could drive him home.

Stevie and Brian were invited in to Gary's room to see Sheba being placated and calmed by a huge bowlful of Pedigree Chum which had now been plopped out into her bowl, schloooooop. Another knock on the door, this time it was Richard Pallister. Then came Alan Greenwood, and here they all were, off-duty, not running, not racing, not training. Gary had been planning this for several weeks – testing the boundaries that held the runners together inside the norms and habits of an athletics club. Fell runners thrived on these boundaries; the sport was nothing if not classless, its uniform (Walsh studded shoes, Ron Hill socks and Helly Hansen waterproofs) made every runner practically indistinguishable from each other, peas of different shapes and sizes squeezed into uniform pods. Runners tended to not even know what each other did outside of the sport; their relationships, their work, their backgrounds all disappeared under the constant hubbub of running chat. This was partly why Gary needed those few weeks off every winter; a chance to take off the costume and work out who he was, away from the madding crowd of the start line.

"Right. You all up for this then?"

They all nodded. Gary bent down and opened the bottom drawer of an ancient chest of drawers under the window. The window looked out onto a shared back garden that had once had a lawn and a flower bed but now had only a square patch of green-grey nothingness littered with cigarette stubs, carrier bags, black bin bags and the rusting engine of a Ford Granada Mk 2, sitting centre stage and at an angle. Gary pulled out a plastic jiffy bag and shook it. It contained an entangled mass of twisty-turny-stringy things.

"Is that it?" said Richard.

"Yeah."

Stevie pulled a face.

"I can't eat that."

"You don't have to eat them. You drink them. In tea. Otherwise they taste horrible."

Gary emptied the bag onto a chopping board next to the sink and began to cut the twisty-turny-stringy things into tiny pieces.

"Can you put the kettle on? It should be full."

Brian checked there was water in the kettle and then pressed its switch, click, with an immediate low hisssss.

"So are we going to get a lifetime ban for this?" laughed Alan. He was joking, but there was enough nervous hesitation in his voice to suggest he was worried.

"Not unless you take it the same day you're doing a race. It disappears from your body within 24 hours, more if you drink a lot of water and piss it out. And besides, who's ever been tested at a fell race? And the thing is, it's probably the most un-performance-enhancing drug you could take. If you took it before a race you'd just stay on the start line laughing at the way your own feet look like blue lizards or something."

Alan laughed again, still nervous.

"Can you get sick from them?"

"Only if someone's picked a poisonous one by mistake. Which means no."

The kettle was beginning to boil. Brian was impatient.

"So you didn't pick them yourself?"

"No. I got them off Ron. Ron who builds the robots. Ron with the 'bastard' tattoo. He goes up to Otley Chevin every morning at the end of summer, he's there at five o'clock in the morning with his dog; you have to go early or they all disappear again into the ground, then you can't see them. There's some cow fields up there, down from The Royalty, he gets hundreds of 'em."

The kettle began to sing. It clicked itself off and Brian carried it across to where Gary was sitting.

"Cups?"

Gary had finished chopping and stood to get several cups from the cupboard above the sink.

"Might need a wash," he smiled. Nobody moved, so he carried on, taking the lid off the kettle before scooping the cut-up mushrooms into his hands and dropping them into the kettle, which he swished around before placing it on the cutting board.

"Give it a few minutes," he said.

An hour later, or maybe two, or possibly three, or was it four, Richard found himself at the local 24-hour garage on the busy Otley Road. He thought that maybe he ought to go back to Gary's house, but he was having such a good time and had never realised how fascinating the forecourt of a garage could be, with all its twinkling, sparkling coloured lights and bags of firewood and multipurpose smokeless fuel with a picture on the sack of a fire that was actually on fire, its flames dancing and twisting.

Back at the flat, Stevie was looking at the wallpaper, trying to make sense of the stories it told, following the unfolding characters and laughing at the intense dialogue as it shifted inch by inch across the wall.

Brian had decided that the record that was playing – 'Caveman Brain', the final track on Gary's battered copy of the English Dogs album *Invasion of the Porky Men* – was actually 'Caveman Brian'. This seemed really unfair. Why had a punk band from Grantham decided to sing a song about him? They'd never even met him. Not that he could remember anyway.

Caveman Brian
You're a sucker to me
A sucker, sucker, sucker
To all society

Alan, meanwhile, was fast asleep on Gary's bed, nestling and snuggling next to a delighted Sheba. It was 6am before he woke with a nagging headache and bits of fur in his mouth.

Outside, the Sunday morning church bells at St Michael's were clanging out-of-tune in the rain and the year was coming to a close. Four runners wandered out into the dawn-dull haze of lifeless Leeds and realised that they weren't going to make the club's morning training run over on Ilkley Moor.

CHAPTER 13

*"...when the sight of the Crags above me on each side, & the
impetuous Clouds just over them, posting so luridly and so
rapidly northward, overawed me; I lay in a state of almost
prophetic Trance & Delight."*
— Samuel Taylor Coleridge

Somewhere in the background, in the world beyond the shared scrappy
back garden with its rotting mattress and polystyrene takeaway
cartons, the Pet Shop Boys were on the radio singing an Elvis Presley
song. Gary looked for a record to play, anything to drown out that
thin-voiced translucent whining. Flicking through the LPs, he came
to the sudden realisation that he hadn't bought a record in over a year.
This came as a shock – either he was getting old or punk had run its
course. The bands he went to see at Adam & Eve's or The Bierkeller
were mostly bands that had formed in the fall-out from the first wave
of punk, then split up and reformed and split up and reformed and split
up and reformed and now had only one original band member. The
cranked-up adrenalin rush of hardcore punk, full speed ahead power
chords and barking dog vocals, was being replaced by a version of
itself with added heavy metal guitar solos. The thrashy, grub-infested
cider punks were getting heavy drug habits and the American version
of hardcore, which came in a package with skateboarding, Converse
All Star sneakers and backwards baseball caps, was swamping the
punk venues. Gary was appalled. The kids were growing their hair and
wearing checked shirts!

He pulled out an album by Discharge, slipped the vinyl from

its card cover and threw side two onto the record player's spindle, simultaneously lifting the needle arm and pulling it across, all the way to track 13, second-to-last, two minutes and fifteen seconds of high-speed noise overload. One riff, two chords, five words.

Free speech
Free speech
For the dumb
Free speech
Free speech
For the dumb

Fast enough and loud enough to gag the Pet Shop Boys, fast enough and loud enough to declare itself a Temporary Autonomous Zone, a space that eluded and dismissed any formal structures of control. A black box to escape into. The only other time Gary could escape into this wild and primitive place was alone on the fells, away from pip pip Greenwich Mean Time and away from the everyday humdrum of the news with its Channel Tunnel project and its three million unemployed and its Hilda Ogden retires and its England cricketer argues with umpire during Test Match and its chart-topping synth duo covering an Elvis song. There was something uncivilised and undomesticated about Discharge's music, something solidly barbaric and feral.

In 1910, experienced fell runner Ernest Dalzell broke the record at the Burnsall Fell Race with what was described as a truly remarkable descent from the summit cairn to the village, with a downhill speed clocked at 21 miles an hour; in his working boots. This phenomenal run wasn't beaten for 67 years and was compared by eyewitnesses to 'a deer, carefree and swift as the footless wind.' Nan Shepherd, in her book *The Living Mountain*, talks of "walking the flesh transparent," meaning that it's possible to become one with the hill, unseparated, enveloped in its wildness through a physical and exhausting connection. This Discharge tune, Gary knew, would hold itself in his head when he slipped out of the front door and ran off towards the Meanwood Valley trail, those two repeated chords playing a basic see-saw pattern he could run to.

Through most of December 1987, Gary didn't train, he ran for pleasure alone. Ran to wake himself up, ran to shake off a hangover, ran to breathe, ran to get out of the house. Come January he'd get back into a twice-a-day training routine, with its Monday track sessions and Wednesday hill reps and weekend races; but for now there was just loud music and strong drinks – he was one party away from 1988, one party over at Nastyville in Woodhouse with its graffitied walls and broken windows and speakers someone had borrowed three summers ago from a sound system in Potternewton Park, five-foot-tall speakers with huge cones protected by thin wire mesh, thick soldered wires connecting to an ancient valve-driven guitar amplifier that powered a cheap record deck with a broken lid. The sound was distorted beyond all reason, effectively turning every record into a blur of excruciating and harsh noise. Which was, of course, how everyone liked it.

Before the party, Gary and a couple of mates met up with a motley group of punks at the bar in Leeds train station, a gathering point for small groups of black-clad lads 'n' lasses from Beeston and Bradford, Halifax and Kendal, some carrying sleeping bags stuffed into carrier bags, some with plastic bottles of cheap, strong lager or cider, some with army-surplus shoulder bags, some with unlaced Doc Marts, all of them appearing from different corners of the station concourse and shuffling, pigeon-toed, as if lifting their feet off the floor to walk was too great an effort.

Four pints of Wifebeater later they all set off up the Otley Road, a straggle of an army, dishevelled, laughing and pushing each other, not an ounce of care in the rotten world. They looked weird and dangerous, and Gary loved that. Students they passed gave them a wide berth and people driving by in cars craned their necks to get a good look at this stumbling, shouting advertisement for multicoloured hair dye. The Kendal punks had become a fixture in the Leeds squatting scene, a small invading force who would send invitations to their mates back in Cumbria to join them; Gary was fascinated by the fact that despite living on the edge of the Lake District none of them had ever been up a mountain. Not that Gary ever talked about running, or mountains, or training schedules or Ron Hill tracksters or compass bearings or the Bob Graham Round or Walsh shoes or Joss Naylor or split times or any of the other things that runners can happily talk about all day. Simply, nobody asked him, so he never told them. Some had seen him out running, and they'd vaguely clocked the shabbily-arranged selection of shields and cups in his room, and some had been surprised when Gary's cousin Jan told them he was actually really good, but running was just something that boring people did, people with boring jobs and boring families who needed to escape their not-so-happy homes for an hour or so every day, people with moustaches and huge watches with lots of buttons, people who would happily wear their dorky, fleecy, breathable, sensible, sweat-wicking, reflective Gore-Tex running clothes even when they weren't running.

By the time they got to the party it was in full flow, a riotous salmagundi of ear-splitting music and illegal substances, people in every room shouting their conversations above the noise and wondering how their drinks were disappearing so fast. Gary cracked open a can of Strongbow cider, took a swig, and dived in.

Five hours later he woke up, gradually, with difficulty.

His mouth was as dry and rough as the floor of a budgie's cage. He tried to open his eyes but couldn't. He tried again, and again. His right arm felt sore. He gave up on opening his eyes and tried to get his bearings. He was lying down. Lying down on his back. He wasn't on the floor, he was on a bed. No, he was *in* a bed. There were sheets over him. He didn't have his boots on. His head ached, a dull fuzz of an ache that ran from temple to crown. There was no music. Everyone must have gone home. What had he missed? What was the last thing he could remember? He couldn't remember.

He tried again to open his eyes. Dimmed lights. High ceiling. A window. A tube, a tube carrying fluid, running from behind him and down to his arm. A clean bed, clean sheets, clean white sheets, voices somewhere, a pull-across tray table to his left. Beyond that, another bed. And another.

He was in a hospital.

Alone, in a bed in a hospital. He tried to lift his head but couldn't. A noise – something close to a splutter – left his lips, and a nurse walked across to him, looming and wearing a puzzled look.

"Oh. Hello."

Gary tried to nod.

"Can you speak?"

Gary shook his head.

"Do you know where you are?"

Another shake.

"You're in Leeds General Infirmary. Do you know where you were last night, before you were brought here?"

Gary nodded and tried to say "party" but only the letter 'p' came out. He tried again, embarrassed.

"P–"

"You came here from a party, your friends brought you in a taxi. You've been unconscious for around 13 hours. Not sleeping, unconscious. A very different thing. We've done some checks and we can't find anything wrong with you – apart from some sort of serious blackout brought on by whatever it was you were drinking or taking last night. Am I making sense?"

"Y–"

"Alright. I'm going to let you rest for a while and then we'll have a look at you. Do you need the toilet?"

"N–no."

"Do you need a drink of water?"

"No."

You're hooked up to a drip which is restoring some of the fluids you lost through vomiting. Do you remember vomiting?"

"No."

"Well, try to keep still and let your body recover and when the consultant comes around we'll have a proper check to see if we can find out what happened. Alright?"

"Y–"

The nurse turned and walked away quickly. Gary closed his eyes. He'd never felt so powerless, so achey, so confused and so alone.

For the next hour, or it may have been five hours, or three weeks, Gary lay with his eyes closed, wide awake, teaching himself a mantra. It was a mantra he invented, there and then, a mantra that said that things would change, that this couldn't ever happen again. The mantra changed every time he recited it silently to himself, but this is what it sometimes said:

I am 21 years old.

I love my running.

I love my racing.

I am really, really, really good at running, and I will not throw it away.

I am 21 years old.

I love my music.

I love my mates.

But I am really, really, really good at running, and I will not throw it away.

I am 21 years old,

And this is a lesson.

The lesson is:

This body is not invincible.

In any sport, the graduation from junior to senior level is often a jump too far. It usually happens right at the time when life's being thrown upside-down and back-to-front, when the world of work is thieving most of your time, when you're learning how to fall in love, when hormones are scrapping it out with training schedules and growing bones, when suddenly there are more important things than tying up your running shoes and going for a run, things like money and alcohol and sex and music and clothes and cars and the gradual looming question mark of what exactly you're going to be doing for the rest of your life. None of this bothered Gary.

Being on the dole meant having time to train, twice a day, meant having time to do bits of cash-in-hand work on the side for his dad, meant space to think and space to drink. Living in a squat meant not paying rent, not being tied to a contract, not feeling responsible for every broken hinge, dripping tap, cracked mirror, faulty light switch and missing pan lid, not feeling like you had to buy a tin of magnolia emulsion to cover up the DESTROY POWER NOT PEOPLE graffiti that somebody upstairs had spray-painted onto the wall in the hallway. Gary was, to all intents and purposes, carefree. He had a room, some money, a dog, a selection of trophies and shields from various races lined up against the wall at the foot of the bed, and a kitbag overflowing with vests, shorts, tracksuits, shoes, socks, caps and a smart new England kit, shorts and vest, white with red panels, clean and folded and packaged in plastic.

And he had a team around him, a team seemingly built in his own image, a team of carefree adventurers who wanted to make their mark on fell running, who wanted to spend every weekend racing around the British countryside in studded shoes, wild camping and drinking until they fell over; and this team, Gary knew, could be the saving of him. The balance of power between fell racing and punk rock had, he now realised – hospitalised, groggy, emptied out and hooked to a drip – swung too far in one direction and now it needed to swing back.

With the help and support of the Pudsey & Bramley team, balance would be restored. No more waking up unable to speak, unable to remember how he got there.

The way it worked was this: Gary's hospital mantra demanded Change with a capital C, but he was never going to be one of those deathbed conversion types; he didn't want to turn over a new leaf or clean up his act or change his ways or start over; he didn't want to rehabilitate or shape up or swear off or (spit) go straight. So he made a decision, a shift of focus, a small sideways step, to immerse himself in the club, in Pudsey & Bramley's wayward and anarchic approach to fell running. He'd spend every weekend with the club, running for the team, drinking with the team, getting into trouble with the team, but crucially not ending up in hospital with the team. The barely-organised rough and tumble of this bunch of 12 or 15 runners had enough of the punk spirit about it to replace the havoc of parties and gigs, but it also offered stability, fitness, purpose and discipline. No drips, no nurses, no hospitals. Change!

1988 and the Mountain Racing World Championship was to be hosted by the English Fell Runners Association up in Keswick in the Lake District, an event that would attract the top mountain runners from across the world – including the seemingly invincible Italians, who had been dominating the sport for several years. Gary had been picked to run for his country in the longer of two races, on an 8-mile route from Braithwaite which climbed around 4,000 feet and took in Grisedale Pike, Crag Hill and Barrow before descending back to the start village. Gary's place in the team hadn't been without its controversy, with several more senior runners vying for a place in what was to be a showcase for the sport. To prepare, the England team management, including Pete Bland and Norman Berry, had arranged a training weekend up in the Lakes with a chance for the selected runners to run around the course, a month or so before the race. On the Saturday evening, team kit was handed out to each of the runners, with the strict instruction not to wear it before the actual race. Coming just a few short months since his hospitalisation, the training weekend proved to Gary that he was fit, healthy, energised, and crucially re-balanced and focussed.

After the weekend, Gary drove home from the Lake District along the A65, through Kendal and Settle and eventually to Gargrave, where he thought he might turn off to Airton and call in at his auntie Maureen's house. The evening sun began to dip and the Shell garage switched on its lights as he passed through Ingleton, the looming shape of Ingleborough rising up to the north. In his rear-view mirror, Gary noticed a police car pulling out of a side road across from the garage, turning to follow his yellow Escort. It hung on a little way behind, cruising at exactly Gary's speed, a steady five-miles-under-the-limit-officer speed. One, two, three miles. Four, five, six. The police car tailed Gary for over ten miles before speeding up to within a few feet of the Escort bumper, switching on its siren and waving Gary over to the side of the road. Miraculously, there was nothing, as far as Gary knew, that was wrong with his car – all the lights were working, front and back, the tyres weren't bald and most importantly the back wasn't full of drunken, dope-smoking, speeding punks.

Both cars pulled to a stop. The policeman pocketed a notepad before climbing out of his car and walking in that way policemen walk (to the tune of *Dixon of Dock Green*) over to Gary's window, beckoning him to wind it down.

"This your vehicle?"

"Yeah."

"You got your documents?"

"No."

"Can I ask where you're going?"

"Home. I've been to the Lakes."

"Where's home?"

"Leeds."

The policeman wrote something in his book. Gary guessed it might just have been, 'Leeds'.

"What you been doing in the Lakes?"

"Running. I've been on a training weekend."

"Training for what?"

"For a race."

"A race?"

"A mountain race."

The policeman didn't bat an eyelid, just sucked his teeth slowly.

"Can I ask you to get out of the car, sir?"

"Er… yeah."

Gary got out of the car. At this point the policeman could get a better view of what Gary was wearing: a black wooly cardigan that was more holes than wool, loosely covering a grey T-shirt that had once been white. The collar had been cut off. The front of the shirt read: NEVER AGAIN above an image of a bayonet stuck through a dead dove. Along the edge of the image was the word 'Discharge'. The policeman carefully read it. For Gary, this was the first time it had occurred to him to wonder what the image was, other than it was the front cover of an album. Gary's black jeans – slightly shiny in the way cotton denim jeans get when they haven't seen a washing machine for several weeks – had holes in the knees that had been patched up several times; various bits of patching remained, layered on top of each other, hanging forlornly at their edges. His Doc Marts were open, their laces trailing.

"Can I see what's in the back of the van?"

"What for?"

'What for' wasn't the answer the policeman was looking for.

The 'sus' laws, introduced to allow police to stop and search at will, was based on the 100-year-old Vagrancy Act and was designed to allow them to stop anyone they suspected of frequenting or loitering in a public place with intent to commit an arrestable offence. In practice it had historically been used widely and indiscriminately and, after rioting across Britain in 1981, the law was repealed. Nevertheless, there remained a belief that police retained the power to stop and search people for no reason other than 'suspicion', especially if you happened to be black, Asian, gay, or simply unusual-looking. Gary was unusual-looking.

"I'll ask you again, sir. I'd like to see what's in the back of your vehicle in order to satisfy myself that you are not engaged in any unlawful or arrestable activities."

As he said this he moved one step closer to Gary, so that the two were now practically nose-to-nose.

"I suppose so," muttered Gary.

They moved to the rear of the van and Gary unlocked the doors. They creaked as they were opened, and a can of anti-freeze that had been rolling around in the back fell out onto the road. The policeman peered in, eyeing Gary's kitbag.

"Show me the bag."

"It's just running stuff."

"I didn't ask what's in the bag, I said show me the bag."

Gary pulled it towards the open doors. It didn't have a zip that worked, so its contents were already erupting from its gaping mouth – socks, shoes, shorts, mostly in hurriedly-rolled balls. The policeman took one look and decided that there was no way he was going to touch any of the filthy scrunches of material he could see.

"Take some things out so I can get a proper look," he deadpanned.

Gary began to pull out various items, dumping them on the van floor. He reached a crisp polythene see-through bag and drew it out. His England kit, ironed, neat, perfect. Its England badge on the chest. Amateur Athletics Association. England. Keswick World Cup 1988.

"What's that?"

"It's my England kit. I run for England."

"You run for England?"

"Yeah."

"You run up mountains, for England?"

"Yeah."

"What's your name?"

"Gary. Gary Devine."

Blank. He was hoping for a Seb Coe or a Steve Cram or some other runner he'd heard of who ran for England, none of whom he'd be able to recognise anyway, he wanted a story to tell the lads down at the station and his kids at home and the landlord at The Bull and Butcher. All he got was Gary Devine in his tattered cardigan and that wasn't enough and he was suddenly feeling like the power was slipping away from him. He fumbled around in his head looking for a way out that might save face. It was the England vest, it had thrown him. He had the abandoned 1824 Vagrancy Act and a uniform and a car with a siren but he could feel it all drifting and disappearing and he started to feel like nothing more than a man on the A65 talking to another man on the A65. And he realised then that Gary was smiling, a big grin of a smile that said, go on then, what do you say now? And the policeman pulled at his cuffs and cleared his throat and all he could think of to say, as he turned back towards his light blue car with POLICE written on the side and a blue light on the top, was:

"Well… don't come back again."

CHAPTER 14

"Over the last 12 months, punk rock has become almost a battlecry in British society. For many people it's a bigger threat to our way of life than Russian communism or hyper-inflation and it certainly generates more popular excitement than either of those. The punk groups have been set upon with words by clergymen and Members of Parliament and this week's papers have carried reports of clashes in King's Road in London and the Teds have promised the punks a battle in Margate later this year.

"Tonight we'll be hearing from Pastor John Cooper, who sees punk as degenerate and evil, and from city councillors in London, in Glasgow, in Birmingham and from Newcastle, whose councils have banned punk concerts. No doubt you'll have your own opinions and we'd like to hear what those are – whether you think punk is a threat to society and whether you think anything should be done about it. You can contact us now while we're on the air by phoning in on 061 236 9494. That number is also included in the Radio Times."

— BBC Brass Tacks, TV punk documentary, Manchester 1977

When you decide to become a punk, Gary had discovered a few years earlier, when you decide to make your hair stick up with a mixture of sugar and water, when you purposely don't fix the holes in your clothes, when you paint anarchy symbols on your jacket and wear trousers that have the legs connected at the knee with bondage straps, then you're basically asking the world to look at you and judge you and make assumptions of you. And most of the assumptions are wrong because they're fed and watered by the *Daily Mail* and by daytime TV chat shows. This can become tedious and tiresome, you can start to feel like a museum piece, a tourist attraction, a part of the cultural furniture. Who wants to end up on a postcard standing next to a smiling policeman underneath a cursive font that reads, 'Greetings from London'?

Which brings us to a small kebab 'n' chips takeaway on a corner of the High Street in Fort William. The town extends its tourist season each year by hosting the Ben Nevis Race in early September, attracting runners from across Britain to race up and down the country's highest mountain. The local shops and hotels fill up, pubs put on extra barrels and the faint of heart lock their doors and peep through the curtains. The owner of the kebab shop fancied himself as more than a purveyor of greasy food, decorating the shop's windows with tartan-edged lettering declaring FISH BURGER CURRY KEBAB above lurid coloured sticky-back photographs of the various foods on offer. In front of the shop, on a small raised courtyard, were two aluminium tables and a scattering of plastic chairs, tempting the 500 or so runners and their families to sit outside in the light grey drizzle and eat their chips from a plate, with a knife and fork, at no extra cost.

The night before the race, late into the evening and the street bustling with pub-crawling locals throwing insults at the sensible runners sensibly sticking to their sensible three-pint rule and leaving the pubs and bars to find something to eat before finding their hotels and tents, a small group of Yorkshire runners headed for the brightly-lit kebab shop. The owner, juggling and jiggling a chip basket in and out of a vat of boiling oil, looked up.

"Evening gentlemen."

"Evening."

The runners squinted at the menu. Paul and his younger brother Brian carried on the argument they'd been having which was something to do with borrowing money and not paying it back.

"Two kebabs please. He's paying."

"No I'm not. I'll have chips with mine an' all."

Richard leaned on the shiny, warm counter display.

"Burger and chips please mate."

Mike took off his glasses which had suddenly steamed up, meaning he couldn't see the menu with or without them. He played safe by repeating Richard's order.

"I'll have that as well. Burger and chips. Thanks."

Gary scoured the rows and rows of words looking for something vegetarian. The more clued-in takeaways up and down the country had started to offer veggie burgers, pale and meatless mulches of unidentified matter made into a burger shape and thrown between two slices of bread. Not up in Fort William they hadn't.

"Do you have anything veggie?"

The owner looked Gary up and down, clocking his English accent and coming to terms with the bright pink spiky hair, the rag-bag holed cardigan and the black jeans held together with patches that read CONFLICT and FIGHT WAR NOT WARS and that image again of the dove impaled on a bayonet.

"I've got chips."

"Are they cooked in vegetable oil?"

"Aye."

The owner suddenly felt inadequate, aware that despite offering a range of dishes from fish to burger to curry to kebab, his choice of vegetarian options was pretty limited.

"I can do you a meatless kebab. Salad and mayo in a pitta bread. You could have that with chips. The curry sauce is meat, so that's out. A chip butty I can do."

"I'll have the pitta bread with chips then. Forget the salad."

There was a minute's silence while the owner threw bread cakes onto sheets of greaseproof paper, rattled the frying chips in their cage and sliced the hot kebab neatly from its glistening, hissing rotisserie. He stood back, arms folded, eyeing up the five blokes, unsure what they were doing here. They didn't look like walkers, most of his out-of-town customers wore distinctive dark blue fleeces and weatherproof trousers, bobble hats and neckerchiefs, checked shirts buttoned at the cuffs.

"You here visiting?"

Richard, ever the polite spokesperson, tired from three pints of something he couldn't pronounce and a seven-hour journey up from Pudsey in the back of Gary's van, smiled and stopped leaning on the counter in a show of alert friendliness.

"Yeah. We're here for the race."

"The Ben?"

"That's the one."

"Just you or all five of you?"

"All of us."

The owner laughed. He'd lived and worked in Fort William for just over a decade and had never once been to the top of Ben Nevis. Actually he'd never been to the foot of Ben Nevis, either. He knew all the stories, of gangs of men hauling a piano up there for charity, of a runner who had raced from the sports field to the summit and back in less than an hour and a half, of the people who die every year attempting to get to the top.

"Bloody hell. You wouldn't catch me up there. Too dangerous."

The Yorkshire contingent laughed, a kind of hollow and insincere laugh that was there just to keep the peace.

"I'm serious," he went on, firmly on home territory now – tut-tutting with the locals about deaths on the Ben and how the out-of-towners underestimate its dangers was a pet subject – "every couple of months there's someone dies up there. Avalanches, storms, falls, exposure. It's not one of your little English hills, y'know."

He laughed, and the world laughed with him, this time with a hint of 'oh no he's going to give us a lecture in mountain-craft, I bet he hasn't even been halfway up the Ben...'

"I mean I haven't been up there myself, but I hear the stories. Any of you lads been up there?"

Gary had, but kept quiet. Mike piped up.

"A couple of us did the race last year."

"Oh well, good on you. How d'you think you'll do this year then?"

Uneasy laughter.

"He'll do well," said Brian, pointing at Gary. "He's our lucky mascot. What d'you reckon Gary?"

The owner eyed Gary while shaking the chips. These lads were obviously having a laugh at someone's expense, and he figured it was probably the punk rocker who hasn't got the gumption to tie his boots. He spoke to Gary.

"How do you think you'll do then, son?"

Gary fidgeted. He wasn't comfortable with these conversations.

"Top ten I reckon."

"Eh?"

"Top ten."

"Top ten?! There's upwards of 500 runners. You're having a laugh."

"No I'm not."

The owner was starting to put sizzling burgers into bread cakes.

"Onions and sauce on your burgers?"

He squirted the ketchup bottle and shook the chips again.

"I'll tell you what. Straight up. Here's a bet for you. If you finish in the top ten –" (by now he was pointing at Gary, wagging his finger) "– if you make top ten you can come in here tomorrow and I'll do ye a veggie supper. Whatever you fancy. How's that?"

"Sounds good."

Everyone laughed, the Yorkshiremen laughed and the kebab

shop owner laughed, and the laughing was weird because they were laughing at different things.

*

The following night, Fort William's main street was livelier and louder. The race had been run, and there was serious drinking to be done – but first, back to the kebab shop. Tartan-edged sign, steaming cabinets, FISH BURGER CURRY KEBAB.

"A'right lads. How did you get on then?"

Same smile, same smell, same sizzle of oil, same glistening kebab.

Gary muttered, "I was second."

The owner laughed.

"Get away with ye's! You were never second."

"I did. I came second, I've come for my veggie supper."

"Get to fuck!"

"I did. I want my free chips."

"You're not getting anything free, you cheeky bam pot. Away and stop wasting my time!"

Gary fished around in his carrier bag and pulled out a folded certificate, with fancy-looking serif lettering and the signatures of the race organisers. He held it up towards the counter, hung it in mid-air between the bubbling, popping fat and the illuminated rows of battered fish and sausages. The owner squinted and looked closely. Three, four, five seconds of near-silence. *Gary Devine, Second Place.*

A few more seconds punctuated by the noise of sizzling oil.

"Here ye go lad," he said, shaking his head, scooping up a shovelful of chips and throwing them into a huge pile on the chip paper. "Now get tae fuck."

That was the previous year, Gary's first Ben, and a realisation that this toughest of races suited him. Last year had been a bright and breezy day – this morning, as the runners left their digs in the town and headed toward the sports field, the weather was atrocious. Cloudy, raining and freezing cold. The rain was falling in heavy, angry drops, and the 500 competitors were still huddled under the wooden sloping shelter of the clubhouse as the tannoy announced starter's orders. Spectators clustered in small blobs, sharing umbrellas, hoods up, hunched.

A voice came on the loudspeaker system:

"The weather at the summit of the mountain is two below freezing, with gale force winds and very low visibility."

As the runners left the show ground – a drenched Scots piper playing them out of the park – the front end of the leading bunch was a who's who of the sport's top athletes: race favourite Colin Donnelly, Ambleside's Mark Rigby and Keith Anderson, Keswick's Rod Pilbeam, the in-form Glossop pair of Whyatt and Prady, Bob Whitfield and the superb Griffiths brothers – Glyn and Hefin – from Wales. Gary buried himself in the huddled group, sensibly sheltering from the driving rain as they left the initial road section and up onto the rocky path winding its way to the Red Burn halfway point. The wind got steadily more vicious, whipping across the face of the mountain as the runners climbed into the thick cloud, clambering up through the sharp, steep boulder-field. Gary found himself in third place as they crossed the summit plateau, behind Colin and Rod, two of the country's best climbers. And in the eye of that awful storm, unable to see further than ten metres in front of him, Gary remembered the kebab shop owner's admonition: "Avalanches, storms, falls, exposure. It's not one of your little English hills…"

And he was right, it wasn't, and this was exactly why Gary loved this race. It represented a kind of pure distillation of British mountain running; its height, its reputation, its history, its bloody-minded nastiness and sense of drama. As runners further down the field reached the Red Burn halfway point, marshals checked their bags to ensure they had full waterproof body cover, gloves, food, compass and whistle. Anyone missing anything was unceremoniously turned back – nobody wanted to see the race become a tragedy. Gary was still in third as they retraced their steps from the remains of the ruined Observatory at the summit, and through the icy rain the front three could make out the gap behind them. Here's what Gary knew: Donnelly was a renowned and fearless descender, but he didn't much like the rain. Maybe it battered his self-confidence, dampened his will to win; this might not be true, but it gave Gary something to hang on to. A crack in the armour. Pilbeam was an incredible climber, especially at home on the relentless climbs of the English Lake District, but if he had a weakness it was in rough descents. To this end he admitted to practising his descending at race pace, and even on his long training runs he had been trying to improve his downhill speed by not holding back, by giving it everything. But still, Gary knew that he could descend a hell of a lot quicker than Rod.

What Gary had in his fell running toolkit, along with a Mars bar, a compass and a photocopied map of the route, was his punk rock 'I don't care' nihilism, a devil-may-care aversion to rationality and level-headedness. He'd got 'so what', and this was where he could use it, here where the leaders approached the zig-zagging path that tumbles off the summit and down, down, down towards Fort William. Gary tried to focus but the rocks were drenched, loose and slippery, the rain was running down his face and into his eyes, and runners on the climb were crossing the path below at regular intervals. He ignored the path and crossed the rough ground between each corner, effectively drawing a straight line across the multiple Z's, heading for the ridiculously steep grassy bank that plunges to the Red Burn before hitting the main path back to base. It was here that he overtook Rod Pilbeam, who was slipping and sliding around down the incline. Don't look back, keep going, focus. The rain continued to fall.

As he hit the final section of road that led from the foot of the mountain to the finish, Gary could make out Colin Donnelly in front, slowing and struggling. This can't be right – Donnelly was invincible, he never struggled. But there he was, drenched and dispirited, reaching the show ground with tiring legs and the grimmest of looks on his saturated face. Gary swept past, into the park and around the last cruel lap of the athletics track, sodden and cold. Colin was just five seconds behind him, the pair of them crossing the line in just over the 90-minute mark. Ninety minutes to climb and descend Britain's highest mountain. Spectators who'd been sheltering in the pavilion emerged to slap Gary on the back and shake his hand, squinting through the rain at this scruff who'd taken on the best and won. Rod finished a couple of minutes later, barely able to speak, the rest of the waterlogged runners lapping that last circuit in various states of desperation and elation. Gary clutched a plastic cup of weak orange juice and waited to applaud his Pudsey team-mates in, knowing that winning the team race – first three finishers to count – was a real achievement for the tiny city-based club. By the time they'd come in around ten minutes later, he had a plan.

"Right then. Prize-giving's not for ages. Shall we go to the pub?"

The prize-giving was held in Fort William proper, in a hall that smelled of formality and tradition. A stage was set with a cloth-covered trestle table, the assorted cups and shields proudly displayed, chairs arranged in perfect lines, portraits of upstanding Scotsmen lining the walls. Pudsey & Bramley did win the team prize, and the announcer's mangling of the club name to 'Pugsley and Brampton' went down particularly well with the assembled fell runners. The main prize of the day was presented by a bemused local dignitary and wife of a race sponsor, who seemed to stand clutching the famous silver cup for an age before Gary reached the stage wearing a grin, a black denim cap, some ripped and grimy black jeans and T-shirt with cut-off sleeves that read EVERY SIX SECONDS AN ANIMAL DIES IN A BRITISH

LABORATORY. He kissed the bemused woman on the cheek, took the cup and stuck it into the carrier bag he was carrying. From there it was, of course, back to the pub before the inevitable return visit to the kebab shop.

*

Jan, Pagan Idols' lead guitarist and singer, had called a summit meeting. It was supposed to be the whole band, but only Gary had turned up, and that was mainly because it was convened in Gary's room. Jan had news, plans, ideas, all part of trying to keep the band together.

"I've got us a gig."

Gary wasn't impressed.

"How can we do a gig? We haven't played for over a year."

"I know. I thought about that. I thought we could call it a reunion gig. Proper, like, telling people and putting it on the posters. So everyone knows."

"Who's everyone? Nobody came to see us before, why would they come to a reunion?"

"Some people came."

"You mean Zip. He's your best mate, that's why he came."

"Dev came."

"Dev goes to everything."

Jan had to admit that a reunion wasn't the best plan to attract an audience. He tried Plan B.

"Do you still have your bass guitar?"

"Erm… I think so."

Come to think of it, Gary hadn't seen his bass guitar for ages. It sat in the corner of the room for a while, then it got lost under a pile of clothes, then it disappeared altogether. Or maybe it was under the bed, or behind the cupboard. How do you lose a bass guitar? It's not like your car keys or a record or a dog collar or a T-shirt or a book or a compass or a five-pound note or a running shoe, it's a four-feet-long piece of wood with strings and knobs and dials. You can't just lose it. But since he had no idea where it was, he let Jan continue.

"I've got some new songs. D'you wanna demo them? They've got a Portastudio in the Armley squat and we could do a proper demo cassette. To sell."

Gary was less convinced about this whole thing now than he'd been when Jan had badgered him for a meeting to discuss the future of the band. The band that Gary thought had split up over a year earlier. Well, not split up. Just disintegrated. Not even disintegrated, just disappeared. Drifted quietly from being a band to not being a band. Which, in punk rock terms, was a sad way to go, but gone it had.

"I've got some other news as well."

Jan's infectiousness was a marvel. He excelled at making purses out of sows' ears and punk rock patches from old material and felt-tip pens.

"I've been asked to be in a band with Spot the Poet. He plays flute and writes poetry; you know Spot?"

Gary couldn't think of anything worse than being in a band with a flute-playing poet. He tried a smile of approval but it just wouldn't come.

"They're called Tree of Life. They do, like, Native American Indian chants and stuff. Weird shit like that. Anyway they've asked if I'll join. And I said, I'm into it if it doesn't mess up what we've got with Pagan Idols…"

Gary realised that Jan was asking for permission to join another band. Actually he was asking, in the politest way possible, to exterminate Pagan Idols. Jan had gone from proposing a reunion to putting an end to the band in about thirty seconds. All he'd had to do was mention Spot the flute-playing poet.

"Go for it," said Gary, "sounds good. I don't know where my bass is anyway. And I can't remember how to play the songs. You're best off with your Tree band."

"Tree of Life."

"Yeah, that. Tree of Life."

And with that the meeting was concluded and Pagan Idols were no more.

*

The Thieveley Pike Race was held at the end of September and started in a field that was famous for hosting TV's *One Man and His Dog*, a show where farmers and shepherds competed to see who had the best sheepdog. The show attracted audiences of over eight million viewers, all keen to watch this pastoral peculiarity, the whistling farmers instructing their dogs ("Come by! Come by, lass!") to wheel and dart and chase until a flock of sheep was corralled into a waiting pen. The 1988 edition of the Thieveley Pike Race was remarkable in that the England team selectors had chosen it as a warm-up race for the England runners who would compete at the Mountain Running World Cup in Keswick just three weeks later.

Hence the flock of runners wheeling and darting around the field before the race, warming up and stretching, included Robin Bergstrand, John Taylor, Malcolm Patterson, Rod Pilbeam, Steve Hawkins and previous winner Dave Cartridge. In the women's race Vanessa Brindle and Jackie Smith were two more of the selected England team to be using Thieveley as a training run. Thieveley Pike is a rough 'n' ready hilltop on the outskirts of Burnley, bleak and open and featureless, and the wider area is peppered with collapsed walls and half-built lanes and the occasional burnt-out car or abandoned armchair. Gary had competed here as a Junior, enjoying the scraggy Lancashire no-frills landscape, so it wasn't a surprise that he hared off at the head of the star-studded field and, against even his own expectations, reached the summit in first place. He wasn't used to this, at least not in races against international runners; he was used to relying on his mad-dash risk-it-all descents, often with a sly quip at the ready for when he passed runners who had beaten him on the climb. "In your own time," was a favourite. "When you're ready," another. Always with a grin, no matter how exhausted – after all, this was fun.

Halfway down the grassy slopes of the race he realised that he was coasting, freewheeling, riding the hill and letting it roll away under his feet. In his local races, the mid-week Yorkshire sprints up and down medium-sized fells, this was his default position, the race going to plan. Work hard to get out in front and extend a lead, then coast. Chat to spectators, even. Have his picture taken. Throw insults at team-mates who were out on the course watching. But here, with a handful of England international runners breathing down his neck? And there they were, not just metaphorically but actually, factually, breathing down his neck, Cartridge, Patterson, Pilbeam, Hawkins, Bergstrand, the heave of their breaths matching the stomp of their studded shoes on the sodden grass. Down to a sharp left turn at a gate, alongside a wall, and hurtling down again at an impossible angle, bodies leaning back, heels digging in on every leap-and-bound. Gary stopped coasting, stopped waiting for the hillside to come up to meet him – he went for it. Dug in and grimaced, stopped the mouthing and the glancing and the pratting around, no stopping for pictures, this was suddenly serious.

It stayed serious all the way to the finish, with Cartridge and Patterson hanging onto Gary's mudprints, busting their guts to bridge the gap between here and there, so very very close, off the fell and onto a path beside a railway line, quick left under the bridge, right along a rough track to where *One Man and His Dog* and all the rest of 'em were gathered peering towards the gap in the fence where the runners suddenly appeared, three of them together, hurtling, tearing, rushing headlong towards a ditch that had to be cleared, one leap, lift and, huueeeggghhh, all the wind in their lungs rushing out as they landed and scrambled to keep running, as they landed to see that Gary had taken the jump in his stride and inched away, further, pulling out every second toward the finish and the applause and shouting and clapping and the whirl of colour and words. Three seconds between first and second. Gary now had around three weeks until the World Cup in Keswick, less than a month to stay fit, stay sober, stay focussed and stay a winner.

CHAPTER 15

1990 British Championship race 4
Eildon Two Hills Race, 23rd June 1990
4.5 miles, 1400ft climb

"That's the thing about running: your greatest runs are rarely
measured by racing success. They are moments in time when
running allows you to see how wonderful your life is."
— Kara Goucher, Olympic long-distance runner

"Have you got any punk?"

The karaoke DJ, clearly in his late forties but dressed like a teenager in baggy shorts and huge Nike trainers, leaned down to try to hear what Brian was asking. Coloured lights swirled around the room and Elton John's recent hit 'Sacrifice' was a down-tempo interlude, a chance to get to the bar before someone had guts enough, or had drunk enough, to get up, choose a song and grab the mic.

"Whaaaat?"

"I said, have you got any punk?"

"Punk? Aach, I don't know. I have The Police. 'Every Breath You Take'?"

"Nah."

"Walking on the Moon?"

"No, not The Police. Anything a bit more punk?"

"Let me think. How about Blondie?"

"Nah."

"'Heart of Glass'?"

"Nah."

"'Denis Denis'?"

"Nah."

"'Hanging on the Telephone'?"

"Nah."

"'Rapture'?"

"Nah."

"'I'm Always Touched by Your Presence Dear'?"

"Eh?"

"One of the later ones. Cracking tune."

Brian was clutching his fourth pint, shouting the odds with the karaoke DJ over the barrage of cheap PA speakers, drunk enough to be trying to cajole Gary up onto the stage to sing. Gary, on his third cider, had agreed on the proviso that it would have to be a punk song. A proper punk song, "Not some baggy-trousered New Wave shite."

Brian left the stage defeated, sank his pint, and asked the table who wanted another one. A singular voice of reason, the only member of the Pudsey & Bramley clan that didn't drink, suggested that maybe they ought to think about getting to bed, since they had a big race tomorrow.

"Bed! We're not going to bed until one of us gets up and sings another one!"

They were camped in what looked like a posh school playing field a mile up the road from the pub, which appeared to be the only open-and-serving pub in the Borders town of Melrose, nestling quietly on the banks of the Tweed. They'd arrived after dark during a prolonged bout of heavy rain, clambered through a gap in a vicious-looking fence, and pitched their tents behind some rugby goalposts. Melrose was the home of Rugby Sevens, a fact which seemed to impress Ady, and Ady alone. He'd even brought a rugby ball with him and was threatening to carry it round at tomorrow's race. Melrose was perfectly positioned at the foot of Eildon's two hills, sparsely-wooded and looming, great pointy-topped things that even in the rain looked imposing. The race route was simple: out and back, up, down, up, down, up, down. It seemed a long way to come for a race, but both Gary and the team knew they had to make an effort to get to the less-fancied races, because if they didn't they'd hear through the grapevine that one of Gary's rivals had got a last-minute entry and won, or that Ambleside had scooped the team points. And besides, besides, besides – it was an excuse for an outing, a weekend club jamboree, Bash Street Kids going wild in the country (and in the Ship Inn, where *Friday Night Is Karaoke Night*).

"Right, me and Danbert have decided we'll do this one –"

Danbert had already been up on the tiny corner stage, two drinks earlier, with a version of 'King of the Road' that included an instrumental break where Dan had swaggered across the pub floor swinging the mic around on its lead. The DJ had raced out to grab the mic before it could become disengaged from the lead and shoot across the bar and into the teeth of the landlord's wife, who was taking a shine to Danbert's performance.

Willie Gaunt, fresh-faced and at the far side of four pints of Younger's Tartan Special, jabbed his finger at the photocopied pages he was holding in a flimsy plastic cover.

"There. 'Fernando'. It's a duet."

Danbert looked nonplussed. Danbert frequently looked nonplussed, and at this stage in the evening, having done his star turn, he was prepared to just nod his head and do what Willie was telling him to do – and if that meant getting up to sing, *'There was something in the air that night, the stars were bright'*, in a pub in Scotland, then so be it. He turned the word nonplussed around in his head, assuming it to be French or Latin, meaning non-plus, no more. He slid his drink away from him across the table and closed his eyes, thinking that if he could just sleep for a few minutes then he might avoid being sick. No more. It was nicer without the lights spinning across every surface in the pub…

Richard shook him by the shoulder, urgent and laughing.

"Danbert! You can't fall asleep! It's your turn again! You're up next!"

Willie was on his feet already, unsteady and grinning from ear to ear.

"C'mon Dan!"

And off they went, on past the tables of bemused locals with their Friday-best shirts and dresses and hairdos and cologne and pints of heavy and glasses of sparkling wine and on up to the tiny stage which was actually just a raised platform where the darts competitions were held. The DJ gave them a nervous wink and handed the mic to Willie; there was only one so they'd have to share. The intro music started, all orchestrated strings and pan pipes, or rather, strings and pan pipes played on a multi-voiced synthesiser by a producer in his home studio in the Cotswolds. The music of the mountains, sweeping and thrilling, and twin-strummed acoustic guitars, and now everyone in the room could picture the video, the four ABBA members around a blazing campfire, all dressed in white, the ABBA girls sitting in that way where the camera could see one full-face and the other side-on. Soft-focus, night-time, huge sparkling stars dotting the sky above them and finally, before the voices come in, the pitter-patter of distant drums. Then Willie and Danbert came in singing, both bellowing into the one microphone, cheeks pressed together, eyes fixed on the lyrics scrolling across a tiny screen, and everybody in the pub, young and old, male and female, began to laugh. A laugh that began as a nervous giggle and soon became a full-voiced, open and communal laugh, shared around the room, northern English athletes and Scottish Border couples, a huge and joyful release of laughter that was soon accompanied by shrieks of encouragement and claps and whistles and a mutual, collective, breathless, red-faced laughter.

Fourth on the list of Melrose's attractions (after the Rugby Sevens Tournament, the Scottish Pipe Band Championships and – seriously – poet Robert Burns' heart in a wooden box) the Two Hills Race was set to start at 2.30 in the afternoon, much to the relief of the Pudsey & Bramley team, who emerged from their tents sometime that following morning with bad breath, headaches, and a memory of singing along, arms in the air, to, *'If I had to do the same again, I would my friend, Fernando'*. Nothing that a full Scottish breakfast and five cups of tea wouldn't try its best to cure.

By mid-afternoon the Greenyards rugby pitch in the centre of town, the race's start, was full-to-bursting with fell runners, the pack boasting several Championship contenders and the best north-of-the-border hill runners including international John Wilkinson and former Ben Nevis winner Dave Rodgers from Lochaber. Colin Donnelly looked fit, focussed and ready, while Shaun Livesey and Andy Peace laughed at Gary's blurred account of the previous night.

The Eildon hills – not high enough to qualify as mountains – were the site of one of Scotland's biggest hill forts, and before that in prehistoric times the site of a number of holy springs. Without the magical aura of mythology the springs were gradually recognised as bogs, either saturating the base of the three hills or running in channels alongside the nearby forest. The stone obelisk on the summit of Mid Hill, the highest of the peaks, tells us that Sir Walter Scott, 'from this spot, was wont to view and point the glories of the Borderland', and the view from the top is, for sure, spectacular. Though had Walter Scott been competing in a British Championship Race he might not have found either time or energy to take in the panoramic views, as the race is a lung-bursting dash from start to finish.

From the gun, the pace was fierce as runners tried to avoid being boxed in along Melrose Main Street and on to the narrow forest track towards the first climb. Gary found a line off the path through scrubby bracken and took the lead over the first summit, but a pack of around ten runners were right on his heels and jostling for position, intense and attentive. The second climb was less steep, and runnable enough to give everyone a chance to regroup before the turn-around. Every time someone dug in and gained a few yards, the pack would push on, closing the gap. Overtaking wasn't easy as the conditions underfoot were slippery after the heavy rain, but still the positions kept shuffling and re-shuffling, with Colin at the front now, unable to distance the field as they plummeted back into the forest. Back to Melrose and the returning dash along the Main Street – they'd been gone less than half an hour – saw the first eight or ten runners still battling it out, into the rugby ground and a final, exhausted lap of the pitch, Colin Donnelly holding off John Wilkinson and a fraction over 30 seconds covering the first eight finishers. Gary crossed the line in fifth place, right behind Shaun and Andy and just 17 seconds behind winner Colin. He was knackered. He couldn't help thinking that maybe last night wasn't such a clever idea. But then again, if he had to do the same again, he would, my friend, Fernando.

CHAPTER 16

"If we believe in nothing, if nothing has any meaning and if we can affirm no values whatsoever, then everything is possible."
— Albert Camus, The Rebel

The debate over who would carry the English flag at the head of the pre-Mountain Running Trophy parade was wisely decided while Gary was in the Royal Oak drinking a quick cider. Two days to go and Gary's priorities didn't include marching along Keswick High Street holding the cross of St George on a pole while people lining the streets clapped and cheered. This pre-show – the multicoloured bunting, speeches over an echoing tannoy, formal introductions, the national teams in their national tracksuits – blurred into a remembered swirl of timetabled, photocopied information sheets that Gary had left back at the hotel. It wasn't that he particularly hated it all, he admitted to being chuffed and proud to be running at this level, against the best mountain runners in the world, in his home country. His dad Hughie was proud, too. So proud that he'd been celebrating for several weeks and was at that moment holding forth in the bar at The George, a 300-year-old coaching house on the main street, each pint of Jennings Bitter filling the gaps between shots of single malt whiskey ("no ice, this stuff's not for watering down").

Not that Gary had ever intended to put his name forward to carry the flag, obviously. If photographs of him waving an England flag had appeared, somehow, back in Leeds, sealed in an A4-size brown envelope and thrown onto a table at Adam & Eve's during GBH's encore, his guts would be as good as garters. He exited the pub and strode up the street, weaving his way between the groups of athletes and coaches, relatives, well-wishers and race officials, finding the England squad – twelve women, eleven men, not counting Gary – ready for the official march-past, a crocodile line of super-fit athletes smiling awkwardly and shuffling in sequence down the pedestrianised centre of the street, wondering what they'd do when they got to the bottom where the pavement meets the busy town-centre road. Gary fished around in his tracksuit pocket and pulled out his scruffy black cap, a tattered and filthy remnant of a punk gig several years earlier where someone had left it on a closing-time table. As the sun tentatively crept out high above the Moot Hall in Keswick, and with just two days to go before his biggest race as a senior international, he put the cap on his head, stuck his hands in his pockets and wished he'd had another pint in the pub. Beside him, Shaun Livesey was thinking much the same thing – he, too, had a notorious dislike of the pre-race ceremonies that attached themselves to international races; so much so that when the official team photograph was being taken before the racing began, Shaun simply disappeared. He timed his reappearance perfectly, just as his race was about to start.

A few months earlier, up the road from Gary's house on the fringes of the student area of Leeds, Roundhay Park hosted a huge concert by Michael Jackson, playing before an audience of over 60,000. You could hear the bass right across the city. Under banks of lasers and through multiple explosions, Jackson repeat-chorused his assertion that, as he said on his new album if only you'd pay attention: *'I'm bad, I'm bad, I'm bad...'*

In this sweep of pop magic, Jackson was co-opting revolt and rebellion and giving it a good tune, much to the distaste of the north Leeds punk squatters who were at the same time organising their annual 'Punks Picnic' on Woodhouse Moor, where fifty or sixty leather-clad drunks could play loud music and consume half a ton of cheap cider in relative peace, bar the odd arrest for disorderly conduct.

Their mantra too could have been 'I'm bad, I'm bad, I'm bad', but late-1980s punk was beginning to seem a bit tame, with many of the British punk bands who'd ripped up the early part of the decade with a combination of volume, speed, swearing, ripped clothing and substance abuse now on the retreat, their brand of nonconformity and insubordination becoming a hard act to maintain. Most of them wilted beneath the prospect of continued international touring schedules involving the same theatre of excess night after night after night after night after night after night.

It's no surprise that the punks left on the scene were beginning to feel marginalised, backed into stylistic corners waiting for the next Conflict gig or hoping Discharge would reform. But Gary wasn't up for retreating just yet. The swarm of US hardcore, with its skateboard and Converse All Star stylings, its super-fast playing (so fast you couldn't, however hard you tried, co-ordinate your dancing feet and arms to the offbeat snare or to the rhythm of the chord changes, so fast it blurred, so fast you couldn't dance to it, just flail and shake your fists), meant that Gary and his mates were forced like wounded animals to harden up their attitudes, play their music louder and faster, drink more, bathe less, take more drugs. Except that none of this chimed with running for England over high mountains.

The 1988 Mountain Running Trophy had been mired in controversy since it had been rumoured that the event would be sponsored by British Nuclear Fuels Ltd, based at Sellafield in West Cumbria. It had been arranged through Danny Hughes, secretary of the World Mountain Running Association, who was employed by BNFL and who was keen to have the company with a reputation for environmental damage associated with a sport with a reputation for protecting and treasuring the environment. Despite a slew of outraged grumbles, not least in the letters page of the official magazine of the FRA, the deal went ahead and the whole shebang was underwritten by a company with a history that included one of the world's worst nuclear accidents and latterly involved the practice of systematically discharging radioactive waste into the ocean. Originally called Windscale, it changed its name in 1981 to try to expunge memories of the 1957 disaster which resulted from a fire in its nuclear reactor, spreading radioactivity right across Cumbria. The joke was that legendary Wasdale fell runner Joss Naylor, who himself worked at Sellafield for several years as a fitter's mate, could be seen on his night-time mountain runs due to his radioactive glow.

In 1983, around the time Joss was completing an epic non-stop 105-mile circuit of the Lakeland mountains, radioactive discharge from Sellafield was washed back from the Irish Sea as slime and remained on the beach at Seascale for six months (no, let's not go beach-combing). In the same year, an investigation found that incidences of leukaemia and other cancers around the site were 10 times the normal, and a report concluded that there was an established link between men working at the plant and cancers in their children. Yet somehow, despite all this, the sponsorship tie-in to the World Mountain Trophy was quickly sealed and delivered. And where was Gary Devine while all this was going on? He was at home in his room, feeding Sheba, turning up the record player and listening to the Flux of Pink Indians' *Neu Smell* EP, a bloody great storm of noise held together by military-style snare drum that begins with a poem, intoned in a mock-northern accent over a background hum of farmyard animals and birdsong:

Can you smell the new smell
Travelling through the air?
Aye, I can lad, it's coming from over there –
Over the hills, down in t'valley
There's new buildings there
There's a nuclear power dumpsite
Someone doesn't care
Parliament says it's safe...

Even as the debate still ping-ponged back and forth, the Fell Runners Association got on with the job of welcoming 170 runners from 17 countries, handing them a surprisingly rain-free weekend and a huge and appreciative crowd of supporters who lined the race routes and summits. Gary was one of four men chosen to race in the Long Race on the Sunday, an eight-mile horseshoe north of Keswick that began with a steep, steep, steep, never-ending ascent of Grizedale Pike, followed by a grassy descent to Coledale and a series of large bumps (Crag Hill, Sail and Barrow... not a prog rock trio) before returning pell-mell to the village of Braithwaite. Three and a half thousand feet of ascent in around 70 minutes. The Italian team were, as ever, favourites – their mountain racing reputation was built on years of victories over continental, mainly uphill-only mountain routes, as well as their insistence on racing in towelette headbands and unstudded running shoes. As much as Gary had felt practically unbeatable over the past few months, he started the race huffing and puffing and struggling to keep pace with the leaders. Up the long climb of Grizedale he watched his England team-mates – Shaun Livesey, Rod Pilbeam and Malcolm Patterson – disappear in front of him, heavy step by heavy step. In front, too, and competing brilliantly with the Swiss and Italian runners, was his Pudsey & Bramley partner Jack Maitland, running for Scotland in that peculiar style of his which was part human, part scuttling crab.

The morning mist that had clung to the mountaintop earlier had blown off and the path down to Coledale at the head of the U-shaped valley was dot-to-dotted by runners stretching away in front. The blue Italian vests were all jockeying for position at the front as Rod Pilbeam, leading the England contingent, stretched out and went with them. Gary was still inside the top twenty or so runners as they reached Barrow and the long breakneck descent to the finish, but even with his reckless and confident approach to downhill racing it was too late to pull back the places he'd lost. He finished 17th, hands-on-knees knackered as he crossed the line, feeling like he'd under-performed. It was some compensation that the England team finished second to the Italians and in front of the much-fancied Swiss, but to Gary this was another international race where team-mates he'd been beating in fell races had outrun him. He tried not to overthink it, instead hitting the Keswick pubs as soon as he'd changed out of his official red-white-and-blue tracksuit and into his black ripped denim, but overthinking it happened anyway. This was the third time he'd run for the English senior men's team and the third time he'd been their fourth counter. It irked him. It nagged at his sense of himself as *not caring*, because he clearly did care. He knew there was a tightrope to walk between, on the one hand, the indiscipline of punk, the wayward don't-give-a-tossness of the music and the lifestyle, and on the other hand the discipline needed to train, to improve, to compete at the highest level. Somehow the balance wasn't right – he felt like he was falling off the tightrope too many times, and climbing back up there was hard, hard, hard.

John Keats was, along with Wordsworth and Coleridge, one of the Romantic English poets, whose radical and celebrated ideas challenged the way we thought about the world around us. All three were mad-keen fell walkers, pioneering the fashion for long and arduous hikes in the mountains, coupling their love of landscape with keen political and societal sensibilities. The punks of their day, they angered critics and mixed their poetry with sexual ambiguity, revolutionary ideals and drug-taking. Coleridge was among the first people to reach the summit of Scafell Pike in the Lake District, while Keats undertook a 600-mile walk around the north of England, Ireland and Scotland, beginning in Lancaster and culminating in an ascent of Ben Nevis.

What the Romantic poets knew, especially in their attempts to

popularise their brave new ideas, was that they were willing to fail –
and this is where poetry meets punk. Johnny Rotten, who had never
sung in public when he was asked to audition for the Sex Pistols
in 1975 by miming along to an Alice Cooper record on Malcolm
McLaren's shop jukebox, admitted to being "terrified", but launched
into an act so grotesquely shocking that he was immediately hired.
McLaren himself used the fear of failure as a defining motivation for
everything he did; his headstone, in Highgate Cemetery, reads:

'Better a spectacular failure, than a benign success.'

Keats wrote:

*'Failure is ... the highway to success, inasmuch as every
discovery of what is false leads us to seek earnestly after what is true,
and every fresh experience points out some form of error which we
shall afterwards carefully avoid.'*

1988 hadn't felt like a particularly good year for Gary, but,
driving back from the Lake District alone, along the road between
Ambleside and Windermere and past Wordsworth's former cottage on
the edge of Grasmere village, he came to the conclusion that, all things
considered, most problems could be solved by listening to some fast,
loud punk music. He stuck on a cassette of Chaos UK's newest album
and fast-forwarded to the third track, a straight-ahead full throttle rant
called 'Indecision'. He turned the volume right up and banged the
steering wheel in time as he drove. There, that felt better.

Can't think what to think
Can't think what to say
Can't seem to live my life
From now or day to day
No, yes, no, yes
Now I'm going mad
At all the fun I've had

It's all going wrong
Me, I don't belong
Crippled by my mind
For something I can't find
Something I can't be
Is it really me?
One day I'll pull through
I'll come back to you
And what will I say
Then what will I say?
Yes, yes, yes, yes: yes!

CHAPTER 17

"We're the poison in the machine.
We're the future; your future."
— Sex Pistols, 'God Save the Queen'

1989 and as the decade drew to a close, it felt like the world had begun to wobble on its axis. Political upheaval was in the air and the Berlin Wall was being hacked into a million souvenirs as young people on both sides of the Eastern bloc danced together in no man's land. Right across Europe, governments changed or toppled, and a velvet revolution brought an end to the communist dictatorships in Czechoslovakia and Romania. The soundtrack was hip-hop, rap, house and rave; and the ten-year dominance of tepid soft-rock, manufactured synth pop and American hair-metal was unceremoniously dumped in skips full of fretless bass guitars outside recording studios. The first commercial internet service providers surfaced and Margaret Thatcher's grip on power was looking tenuous, even as her heavily-made-up face became ever more demonically fixed. Change!

Gary's world continued to shift gradually away from the shock and immediacy of his punk rock gigs and towards the punk rock immediacy offered by his rag-tag running club and their assault on the sport of fell running. Fell Runners Association treasurer Kevan Shand, a tough, tanned builder with a moustache and a mullet, had worked tirelessly in the sport for many years and was moved to write at the start of the 1989 season:

'Pudsey & Bramley – the fell club of the future. They are all young lads. Not a codger in sight…'

Somehow this out-of-step scramble of a team were starting to win things, and with each race their unholy camaraderie grew stronger and stickier. As soon as the season's Championship races were announced, the core of the team – around ten or twelve runners – committed themselves to getting to the Championship starting lines and staying until they were thrown out of the post-race pub. This disparate gang (mechanic, bottle factory foreman, caretaker, musician, builder, printer, surveyor, etc etc etc etc) trained together two or three nights a week and raced almost every weekend, piling into shared cars and vans and heading to the Lakes, to Scotland and Wales, to the Peaks and the Dales. They lived, breathed and ate fell running, sleeping in their cars and in tiny tents, wild camping in parks and beside football pitches and on traffic roundabouts. Inevitably it all paid off, all of them improving as mountain runners by dint of their increased competitiveness, their shared will to win. But more than the training and the racing, it was fun, the kind of laugh-out-loud sense-of-belonging fun that Gary had found in punk. Back home in Leeds, the punk scene was slowly, slowly moulding and furring, decomposing and decaying. The winter of 1988 brought with it an influx of heroin into the Leeds squatting scene, and when two lads who Gary knew overdosed and died, he moved a few steps further away from the noise and bluster of punk rock. He still loved nothing more than playing something terrifyingly loud and fast by Amebix or Broken Bones or Discharge, still stamped along to the records, still mouthed the words and still felt it hitting him right there in his chest. But it wasn't the same – how could it be? It wasn't new any more, it didn't shock people any more.

And so Gary took to the fells, hammering out the 1, 2, 1, 2, rhythm in his stride, joined along the way by a small and odd-shaped army of team-mates. First up for 1989, the early-season Chew Valley Skyline, a wintry shivering slogging bog-trotting grough-hopping long-haul drag of a grind that sets off from the middle of nowhere before touring the further edges of nowhere and back, in a mighty loop of frost-bitten moorland. Thirteen miles and 2,000 feet of climb, early enough in the year to guarantee either snow, ice or freezing stair-rod rain, the race set off beside a frozen-solid reservoir and climbed for several miles towards the gloomy and desolate landscape of Saddleworth Moor made infamous as the burial ground for the Moors Murderers' victims. One of the bodies – of 12-year-old Keith Bennett – has never been found, and once you've mustered enough morbid curiosity to look at the area of the burials on a map, it's hard to walk or run across the rough and featureless moor without a feeling of utter desolation.

Thankfully from there the race route turned back and headed southwards, descending and climbing along peat-coloured streams that have gouged out channels that rip roughly across the land, across a thin icy covering that breaks as you run through it, slicing at your ankles until they bleed. The last few miles were a skyline trog and a welcome plunge back to the start. Chew Valley Skyline was always a hell of a race, but despite the presence of locals Mark Whyatt and Andy Trigg (tall, solid, tough as nails, Trigg being especially suited to these onerous courses) and the up-and-coming John Taylor from Holmfirth, Gary won the race by just a handful of seconds. That early-season victory set a pattern of race wins that would typify the season, earning him a full-page feature in the *Yorkshire Post*. Interviewer Eileen Jones finished the piece with a quote from Gary: "That's what I love about the fell running scene – the atmosphere and the people. And in the end it's the team effort that really matters."

Calder Valley, steep-sided and threaded by railway, canal and river, is a valley strung through with disused mills and the dark grey remnants of a powerful and lucrative industrial past, now home to outsiders and nonconformists, radicals and free-thinkers, people who escaped the shiny new shopping-centre cities and found cheap homes in the dying towns along the valley. The Calder Valley Race, 14 miles and 3600 feet of climb, criss-crossed the settlements and weaved around the upland farms, up there with what Ted Hughes called "the sluttiest sheep in England". Another tough one, climbing up and over both valley sides and taking in Stoodley Pike, a magnificent stone skyline memorial built not to commemorate victory in war but to commemorate a war's ending; fitting that this valley full of peace activists should have a monument predating their arrival.

As the year progressed, Bingley Harriers runner Ian Holmes, short, light and lean, was slowly moving up the results, race to race, from the teens to top ten, a place at a time. Getting better all the time, and there at Calder Valley hanging on desperately to Gary for five, six miles before quietly drifting backwards, losing minutes by the end, by the final climb into a vicious wind – Gary a comfortable winner, with time to get changed into something warmer as the rest of the field came across the finish line.

Then the dry weather blew in, a few weeks without rain, firm underfoot, speeding up the courses. Simon's Seat Race again, where the race winner's trophy was a polished wooden toilet seat. Gary had made this race his own, winning it several times on the trot, always against strong opposition – just up the river from Bolton Abbey, it was easily get-to-able from Lancashire and Yorkshire. This year saw a smattering of international runners – Andy Peace and Mick Hawkins of Bingley, Greg Hull of Leeds, and in Pudsey & Bramley's colours, Willie Gaunt, a class athlete learning how to race on the fells. Willie came from a family of wool and worsted manufacturers, fine cloth for fine suits since before the war, and drove a knackered white Peugeot. He wore John Lennon specs and, as the P&B team found out in several pubs on several away-day trips to races, seemed to have a knack for inviting trouble from locals. Locals who took umbrage to someone with an educated accent and small round spectacles. Nevertheless, he was a mad and foolhardy daredevil descender, throwing his bony frame down rocky scree and somehow reaching the bottom on his feet.

Despite the close attention of Peace, Hull and Hawkins (in that order, neatly-packed as a trio of BBC children's puppets) Gary pulled away on the descent from the summit's rocky outcrop which drops steeply through rough heather to meet a drystone wall. Gaining twenty seconds or so, he spent the short climb back towards the skyline listening to the heavy breathing of the chasing pack getting closer by the second, until reaching the ridge, he could let go and hurl himself down the rough track with barely a look back. Easy. Another one in the bag.

After a strong second place behind former winner Shaun Livesey at the Three Peaks Race, a classic 23-mile Yorkshire race up and over Pen-y-Ghent, Whernside and Ingleborough, Gary and the Pudsey & Bramley gang headed up to Kaim Hill to contest a Championship race, an out-and-back up-and-down sprint from Fairlie, perched on the west coast of Scotland. Both Gary and the team won, spending a fair portion of the evening avoiding being beaten up by territorial drunks in the local pub. When Irish poet W.B. Yeats came up with his famous line, 'There are no strangers here; only friends you haven't yet met,' he clearly hadn't been on a tour of fell race venues with a bunch of amateur runners from Yorkshire. They were a peaceable bunch – skinny, good-humoured, not a tough nut among 'em. How they ended up in a variety of incidents with locals can probably be put down to a) alcohol and b) fear of the outsider, with gangs of villagers drunk on bravado reverting to the cultural dog-fight mentality they'd learned from their dads and their dads' dads before them and their dads' dads' dads and back through a history of dads.

Punk, despite the later aggressive look of its studded jackets and Doc Mart boots, wasn't built on a culture of aggression or toughness; it sprang from the dandified, mix 'n' match, his 'n' hers clothing stitched up by Malcolm McLaren and Vivienne Westwood. From their King's Road base they plotted a revolution in style and attached it to a soundtrack that matched; the style was sexual, home-made and cheap, even though the clothes they sold cost an arm and a leg. The secret was that, with both the fashion and the music, you could do it yourself

– anyone could cut holes in a jacket and fasten it back together with safety-pins, anyone could learn three chords on a cheap electric guitar. It was a manifesto for inclusivity, and it defiantly rejected rock 'n' roll's previous tough image of the surly loner ready to ruck. Nevertheless, for its first two years, punks across Britain were chased, attacked, beaten up and knifed by gangs of teddy boys, skinheads and bikers. Punk rejected homophobia and welcomed androgyny, and broke the mould in championing women as musicians – gone was the age of beautiful and fragile singing puppets, here were Siouxsie Sioux, Poly Styrene, The Slits, Chrissie Hynde and Patti Smith.

Punk was also by its nature political, and from the off it railed against racism, sexism and violence – even the most loud and angry of the first wave of punk bands were avowedly anti-war:

Religion instigates this hate and war
As another victim life escapes through gunshot wound
A stray bullet kills an innocent child
Nothing's gained and nothing's solved
    — Discharge, from *Fight Back* EP, 1980

The years that followed, though, under the yoke of Margaret Thatcher's ruthless economic policies, unfolded to become a decade of self-interest, arrogance and ego. The waste of human lives that was the 1982 Falklands War was followed by the bitter and divisive attack on the working-class miners and their communities in 1984, ushering in a society that seemed to be drunk on conceit and pretence. It was perhaps inevitable that punk's initial calls for equality, fairness and peace would be replaced by a more aggressive, louder, faster, harder version of itself. Enter The Exploited, initial standard-bearers for a nastier punk rock, a punk rock that came out fighting.

Chaos, chaos, chaos, chaos
Don't give a fuck
Disorder
Disorder
Disorder
Disorder
Disorder
Disorder
Disorder

    — The Exploited, 'Disorder', 1982

The Exploited soundtracked a different set of punk attitudes, an antidote to the shiny, office-block, Filofax, Duran Duran world they saw around them. And as the punk squats discovered harder drugs, it also discovered a belligerent, combative, 'everybody hates us' hostility.

For all his cheek and bravado, Gary wasn't a fighter. He watched the changing scene around him at home, saw the holes punched in doors, felt the tension, saw the drugs and the come-downs and the inevitable fall-outs and bust-ups, and began to wonder where he fit into it all.

It was a mid-summer morning, a Leeds red-brick terrace, sun barely up and absolute quiet in the house. No taps dripping, no floorboards creaking, no hinges squeaking. The morning after a long night, empty cans scattered around the house's front room, curtains closed, a sleeping stranger on the sofa covered in a stained quilt. Silence. Through a gap in the curtains, a sliver of sunlight cut a line diagonally across the room, tiny strands of dust floated through it and disappeared. Upstairs, two floors, four rooms and seven people, all dead to the world, cocooned and cosy and untroubled. Gary's room was first left off the upstairs hallway next to the toilet, one huge window facing the back and looking out towards Meanwood, its tumbledown ridge and its scraggy woods and fly-tipped fields. Curtains open and light streaming in. Still silence.

Then a flick, flick, flick sound. Sheba the German Shepherd, older now, calmer, quieter, her ears flicking and twitching, attuned to the sounds of someone approaching the house. She raised her head and her ears twitched again, this time quicker. A faint scratching coming from the front garden –

WOOF

Sheba punctured the quiet with one deafening bark, left it a second, two seconds, then

WOOF

Again, louder, and again

WOOF

WOOF

And on and on until Gary raised his head from his pillow and squinted and shouted

"Sheba!"

Because obviously there can't be anyone at the front door, it's barely light, it's Sunday, and what time is it anyway –

WOOF

WOOF

WOOF

Sheba's alarm clock was off and ringing now, with no snooze button, no volume control, and no matter how many times Gary shouted "Sheba!" she wouldn't shut up, she wouldn't shut up because someone was IN THE HOUSE and coming up the stairs –

"Boys and girls, open up!"

Shouted, deep voices, gruff and demanding and loud and matching Sheba bark-for-bark.

"Up and awake everyone!"

WOOF

"We have a warrant to search –"

WOOF

"– your rooms and we have authority to seize and retain goods and articles we deem suspicious –"

WOOF

"– knock knock ladies and gentlemen, stay in your rooms, up, up, up! And chain the dog! Whoever has the dog, chain it!"

Sheba was twisting and turning in a frantic loop of chase-your-tail, occasionally jumping heavily at the closed door. Gary was up, over to the window, seeing the back garden below empty, and grabbing two, three, four potted cannabis plants that sat in an untidy row on the windowsill, grabbing and throwing each one in turn, out and down into the garden as far as he could reach, throwing underarm through the half-opened window. Each pot hit the mud 'n' mess of the garden with a thud, one or two of the pots broke, and the plants lay sprawled like triffids, limbs splayed out and twisted.

Behind him, Sheba's bark turned into a growl, a long, nasty, hateful growl – she didn't like the voices outside, the commotion, the doors banging, the arguing, the cries of "Fuck off!" and "Leave me alone!", she didn't like this sudden disruption. Gary closed the window, leapt towards Sheba and grabbed her by the neck, calming her down. She stopped barking. He clipped a lead into her collar and whispered into her ear and she slumped, shivering. The door opened a fraction and dark-suited bodies yelled through the gap.

"Tie it up! Tie it up and keep it quiet!"

Gary scanned the room. Through the crack in the door he could see and hear his room-mates being marched along corridors and hallways and down the stairs, grumbles and arguments and swearing, stumbling feet and snatches of shouted orders.

"Lady officer needed up here!"

"Got something in the front room, Super!"

"Bathroom clear! Toilet clear!"

Four officers gingerly entered Gary's room, all eyes on Sheba, who began to bark again, held tight on her lead, panting and straining and whimpering. The officers – three men, one woman – looked around the room as Gary pressed his body against Sheba's, quieting her, gradually calming her down. Gary waited until there was a pause in the ongoing uproar, a moment's silence in the thudding commotion and the heavy, tense presence of four police officers, and said simply,

"Can I help you?"

Everyone in the house was cautioned except Gary and *(name withheld)* who lived in the next-door room. The cannabis plants weren't Gary's – they were there because he had the room with the south-facing window – he never touched the stuff. It made you slow, dozy and dumb, when all he wanted was to be fast, aware and alert. Any lingering smell the plants might have given off seemed to have been covered by the combined smells of dog breath, unwashed running kit and the small mountain of running shoes piled behind the door.

What Gary couldn't work out was how *(name withheld)* had avoided arrest – Gary knew for a fact that he had several bags of various pills and powders kept in the top drawer of a bedside cupboard, the only piece of real furniture in the room. Everything else in there was in piles – bedclothes, shoes, jackets, towels, magazines, records, untidy toppling piles of stuff that bled into other stuff. By the time Gary arrived back from the police station, officially released without charge by a duty officer who clearly didn't believe his claim to be drug-free, *(name withheld)* was already home, smoking a joint and watching a repeated episode of *The Sweeney* on the tired TV in the downstairs room, feet up on a chair, scratching his groin.

"A'right Gaz."

"A'right. What you doing back here?"

"Didn't find anything. Dozy bastards."

"But you had all sorts in there didn't you? Loads of whizz and blow."

"I pushed it to the back of the drawer when I heard the downstairs door being forced. I think they were too busy worrying about Sheba!"

"Yeah, right. They left her locked in my room in the end."

"Want a drag on this?" He offered Gary a spliff that was huge, untidy, limp and damp.

"Er, no. I don't smoke remember?"

"Oh yeah. Forgot."

"Anyway I'm off for a run."

"You what? Off for a what?"

"A run."

"Oh. Right. That's what I thought you said."

He blew out a chestful of smoke that must have somehow been held in there while he was having the conversation and switched his gaze back to *The Sweeney*. Gary ambled off to his room, where he could hear Sheba whimpering on the other side of the door to welcome him home.

A month later and Gary was lying in the bath on a Sunday afternoon after a long training run around Ilkley Moor with the rest of the Pudsey & Bramley team. They'd met at Dick Hudson's, an isolated pub on the southern edge of the moor, and covered a 16-mile circuit, through peat bogs, over rough heather, across springy turf, through a dense managed forest and along well-walked paths that stretched from Silsden across to Menston, a huge swathe of common land etched with trails and tracks. The team were fiercely competitive and still improving, with these Sunday runs often coming after Saturday races. Gary knew he was over-racing but couldn't help himself – his nihilist version of punk, his ideology of 'have a good time and stuff the rest' – didn't sit easily with his running, where being part of a team gave him purpose, security and impetus to improve, above and beyond his own personal will to win. When naturalist Charles Darwin was about to publish his controversial book *On the Origin of Species*, he escaped from his home in rural Kent – and from the eyes of expectant newspaper reporters – and travelled north to Ilkley. On the day of publication he was taking the spa waters in a bathhouse perched up on the northern slopes of Ilkley Moor. Darwin's theories, though ridiculed and lampooned at the time in the popular press and by religious fundamentalists, became accepted and revered: he maintained that over the long history of humankind (and animal kind), "those who learned to collaborate and improvise most effectively have prevailed." At the recent Otley Chevin fell race, Gary had won and Pudsey & Bramley had taken the first four positions – six of the top ten were in P&B colours. He wondered if, one day soon, the rest of the team would start to catch and overtake him; before deciding that no, they wouldn't.

This was just one of the things going through Gary's mind as he lay in the bath, soaking away the hard miles. The other things?

a) Margaret Thatcher had now been in power for ten years. Watching his dad struggling to make ends meet with the building business, Gary loathed the woman with a passion.

b) There was a theory, lately passed on to him by his team-mate Jack Maitland, that almost all high-performing athletes have some kind of troubled background which spurs them on to win, be it a broken home, an abused or deprived childhood or a death in the family. Since Gary's mum and dad had split up he wondered if this applied to him. He still visited his mum once every week or so and still took his dirty running clothes round to be washed; and his dad Hughie still turned up at races to watch and encourage him. So he decided that, no, it probably didn't.

c) Then again, what about the official from Bingley Harriers who'd turned up at his front door when he was just a kid, warning him about racing in professional competitions and threatening him with disqualification of amateur status? That, surely, was a motivating factor, a constant reminder of the pettiness and narrow-mindedness of the establishment... a short, sharp prick in the hippocampus, that small squidgy bit of your brain that catalogues memories. He decided that, for the purposes of a good story, yes, it probably was.

d) Scottish punk-noise band Toxik Ephex (Gary had their first single, 'Punk as Fuck') were coming to the Duchess of York, supported by Huddersfield's The Instigators. The Duchess of York was Leeds's best venue, a dark and dingy, strangely-shaped pub with a sticky carpet and a tone-deaf front-of-house soundman. The cider on tap was weak but it was cheap – as were ticket prices. He was looking forward to this one. Some band from America called Nirvana were playing there sometime soon, a couple of the Meanwood punks had said they were worth seeing. Gary decided they were probably long-haired hippies pretending to be punk and erased them from his memory.

e) ... how was it possible for *(name withheld)* to have so many bags of pills and powders in his room and escape arrest?

The 1989 fell running year came to a close with Gary finishing second in the British Championship to three-times champion Colin Donnelly, the two of them way ahead of any of their rivals. Gary was crowned English Champion and the team, Pudsey & Bramley's ragged bunch of misfits and miscreants, scooped both the British and English team championships. It was a good season's work for Gary, and proved that the shift he'd made in his attitude to racing – and specifically his attitude to waking up in a hospital on a drip and without a clue as to how he'd got there – was working. The rough and tumble of regular weekend trips to races had, to an extent, replaced the rough and tumble of regular jaunts to punk gigs in places like Oldham, Nottingham and Sunderland. Not completely, though. Gary's dad Hughie was now drinking more, falling over more and having to be gently coaxed out of pubs at closing time more. His white van was still a popular choice of transport to races, but by the time the team had registered and changed, Hughie would be in the pub sinking a bitter with a whiskey chaser. He was garrulous, funny and warm-hearted and consequently he made friends easily. One thing Gary had taught his dad was to be open-minded; he'd think nothing of piling seven or eight punks into the back of the van and treating them all to an afternoon at the very upmarket Angel Inn, in the quiet village of Hetton, demanding fine wine and making sure the locals were watching the spectacle of a bunch of spikey-haired city kids bringing down the tone of the place.

The last race of the year for Gary was the Winter Hill race. It was a race he loved, and he was determined to win it, setting off at a cracking pace at the head of a group containing Andy Styan, Keith Anderson, Graham Schofield, Ray Owen and Richard Pallister. By the time they'd hit the first descent from the hill's flat plateau to its lower slopes, he'd shaken almost everyone off. At this point, though, only a handful of miles in, it was clear that Ambleside's Keith Anderson was doggedly sticking with him. Anderson was relatively new to the sport but was proving to be an outstanding athlete. His talent was in downhill racing – he could stretch out on the roughest of descents and negotiate any amount of boulders, mud and scree, his tall slight frame leaning slightly backwards to dig his heels into whatever was underfoot as he moved at breathtaking speed. Gary had always relied on his downhill pace and agility, but he knew that Keith was getting a reputation as the runner most likely to plummet fastest down breathtaking slopes.

Gary was aware that Keith would be a definite contender for next year's Championship and was anxious to find a way to race against him, to exploit any weaknesses. After the long descent from the Winter Hill TV mast, and with around four miles to go, Gary attacked the next uphill mile with a vengeance. This section is the heart of the race – eight miles in, the fun wearing thin, you're tired and you're thirsty – and the race route heads up onto Rivington Moor and to the small valley cut by the River Douglas. It's not terribly steep or long, but in bad weather and with terrible underfoot conditions (and the race could always guarantee both) it was an energy-draining, strength-sapping grovel through sodden moorland with hidden ditches, mud-pools and peat bogs. Gary gritted his teeth and got stuck in, focussing only on his own race and unaware that Keith was done, spent, hands-on-hips stumbling to try to stay in touch, looking behind him to see if he'd be able to hold second place. Gary's win – over two minutes up on Anderson at the finish – signalled not just the finale to a good year's running but a taste of what could be an even better year to come.

And to crown it all, Christmas came early at Gary's house: with frost spidering the pavements and the two-bar electric heater left on overnight (the electric meter was fixed, stopped in its tracks by a small black plastic transformer that was bought from one of the Woodhouse squatters for the price of a round at the pub), the gently breaking dawn was rudely interrupted by the smash boom blast crash slam crack bash of twelve police officers wrenching the front door off its hinges with a battering ram. This time Gary had nobody else's potted plant collection on his windowsill, and Sheba, once she'd got over the initial shock, was relatively subdued, as if she'd seen it all before and was used to this kind of thing and could take it or leave it and didn't know what all the fuss was about. But once again, when the explosion of morning had given way to the aftershock of the afternoon, Gary was surprised to find that *(name withheld)* somehow, once again, had been released from custody within an hour or two and without any charges being brought.

"So, how come you got away with it this time!?"

"Hid my stuff again, they didn't find any of it. Idiots. They're stupid, you know that don't you? Just missed it. Looked in the wrong places."

"Again? What, loads of pills and tabs and weed?"

"Again. Ridiculous isn't it?"

"Yeah."

"I'm on a lucky streak, that's all. Lucky me."

"Right. Suppose so. Anyway. I'm off for a run."

"A what?"

"A run."

"Oh. That's what I thought I heard you say. Seeya."

*

The following week, Gary moved out of the house.

CHAPTER 18

1990 British Championship race 5
Snowdon Race, 28th July 1990
10 miles, 3200ft climb

"They always say time changes things, but you actually have to change them yourself."
— Andy Warhol

Somewhere in the bottom of Gary's kitbag, swimming around with the discarded race numbers, single socks, waterproof leggings and loose safety-pins, was a creased and weathered copy of *The Fell Runners Handbook & Fixtures Calendar*, an A5-sized handbook of the year's races, detailing every FRA-sanctioned event. It was the fell runner's bible, a densely-typed litany that measured out the months in sparse, functional chronology. A triumph of no-frills classification; straightforward and convenient. (As Dead Kennedys lead singer Jello Biafra sang, with as much irony as he could muster, "Give me convenience or give me death!") The Calendar came with FRA membership and acted as a secret passage to a hidden world, detailing times and places where people would gather in clumps, strip down to vests and shorts and head en masse up the nearest hill.

The entire sport was a huge mystery that took place away from the public eye, an enigmatic and underground affair that had its own codes and customs. Where punk rockers gathered outside train stations and begged for small change in market squares, their clothes and hairstyles screaming 'look at me!', fell runners ran away from the cities, hiding themselves in the hills and valleys, searching out the most remote of horizons. The 1990 *Calendar* listed over 250 races, almost all of them unknown outside the sport's cliques and clubs; well, *almost* all – three races had, through reputation, renown and rumour, climbed out of the *Calendar* and into the public consciousness: Ben Nevis, Snowdon and the Three Peaks. Ben Nevis simply because it was Britain's highest mountain, Snowdon because of its status as a tourist attraction, and the Three Peaks because of its standing as a popular walkers' challenge. All three races played a significant part in Gary's year, for various reasons, and all three came as a package of tradition and mythology.

The records for both Snowdon and the Ben were held by Kenny Stuart, a Lakeland gardener and incredible mountain runner who had set times in the mid-1980s that many saw as unbeatable. Running at Snowdon in 1985 he had fought off the challenge of Italy's legendary Fausto Bonzi, the previous year's winner, completing the race to the summit and back in little over 62 minutes. His time for running up and down Ben Nevis in 1984, including the out-and-back run from Fort William to the foot of the mountain, was 1 hour 25 minutes. The choice of both Snowdon and Ben Nevis races as counters in the year's Championship seemed strange: Snowdon was an international race with teams invited from the four home countries as well as from across the continent, while Ben Nevis was a race that was notoriously difficult to get an entry for; it regularly reached its capacity almost as soon as the race's opening date for entries was announced.

Colin Donnelly, in a commanding position in the Championship, had decided early in the season that he would avoid racing at Ben Nevis – he could run at Snowdon and that would be his medium-length counter (there had to be at least one of each distance category in the final four races completed). He hated the Ben, disliked the officious way it was organised by its ageing committee, and had vowed never to race there again; and as long as he made sure to run well at Snowdon he could aim to secure his fourth successive British Championship victory. Then, for reasons best known to himself – Colin was famously taciturn – he accepted an invite to run the 42-mile Davos mountain marathon in Switzerland the same week as the Snowdon race. Not to worry, he'd just race at the Ben. Except that entries to the Ben Nevis race were closed, all 600 places being filled several months earlier. Colin would have known this, but he assumed that, with the stakes being so high and considering his own high profile within the sport, he'd be able to secure an entry to the Ben Nevis race.

Colin had won the Snowdon race in 1988, and it suited him. A short run from the centre of Llanberis, past terraced housing and eventually leaving the tarmac track and heading straight up the mountain. The race is fast and relentless, and especially strange in that for much of the way it mirrors the route of the famous Snowdon Mountain railway – part of the race's notoriety outside fell running circles is possibly in watching human beings climbing a mountain faster than a steam locomotive. It's a race that can leave you with blisters, the descent a continuous gradient retracing that same unforgiving loose stone track, and there's often a queue of walkers at the mountaintop standing in line to touch the summit cairn – around 350,000 people every year make the journey to the highest peak in Wales and England.

Not being selected to represent England at the 1990 race meant that Gary would be running in his club vest alongside the international vests of the four home countries and Italy – it also meant that the vital Championship points would be hoovered up by the international runners. The journey to Llanberis – six runners in the back of Hughie's van – was spent trying to play cards as his dad went full throttle down the A55 North Wales coast road. These journeys were never a great start to a day of intense racing, and so, still feeling slightly sick, Gary set off at the start in Padarn Park surrounded by runners wearing their national colours and a large crowd of supporters waving small Welsh flags. Conditions were good for running – clear and not too warm – but in many ways it was a race Gary could never love, and with its lack of twists and turns or varying terrain it was just too… obvious. A proper runner's course, not a fell runner's hotchpotch of scree and grass, stream jumps, boulder clambers and navigational choices. In short, it wasn't an adventure, it didn't have the ability to surprise. Still, to win the Championship meant being able to tackle whatever was thrown at you, and as Gary sprinted through the streets of Llanberis to finish in 9th place, just under 70 minutes later, he was thankful he'd managed the downhill without falling or blistering.

Colin's absence at Snowdon meant that, with one race remaining, Gary was now in pole position in the Championship, just one point in front of Shaun Livesey. Like Colin, Shaun had neglected to enter the Ben Nevis race; the Fell Runners Association was already beavering away trying to persuade the Ben's organising committee to change their position and allow these two elite runners to race. There was an irony in the FRA petitioning the Ben Nevis organisers to allow Colin Donnelly to enter the race, since Colin had vowed never to take up membership of the FRA, declaring it an organisation only for English runners; the added itch of Colin's well-known criticism of the Ben Nevis organisers probably didn't help.

Over the few weeks between the Snowdon Race and the Ben, messages and phone calls criss-crossed the Scottish border and rumours of both a change of heart and a steadfast refusal somehow filtered through to runners at club level. Gary was reasonably confident about doing well at Ben Nevis, though he readily admitted that Colin Donnelly was in the better form. Shaun Livesey had a reputation for tailing off or getting injured as each season progressed, his aggressive training schedule being literally exhausting – upwards of 100 miles every week throughout the year.

Earlier in the year, Gary and Shaun had battled it out at the classic Three Peaks race in Yorkshire. Known as 'the Marathon with Mountains', the Three Peaks is a recognised walking challenge undertaken by around 200,000 people each year, who all aim to complete the course in under 12 hours. Elite male runners finish the race in under three hours; elite women in a little over.

Some thought it self-destructive to compete at the arduous Three Peaks Race so early in the Championship season. The new format of the British Championship had been introduced to counter claims that the previous configuration – six best races to count out of nine – was too arduous and prevented runners from properly preparing, or hampered runners wanting to compete successfully in international races. Colin in particular had complained bitterly about the way the FRA organised the Championships, grumbling about the races starting too soon after the cross-country season and, for good measure, complaining about the lack of any financial help towards getting to races. This new arrangement should have given all the elite contenders space and time to properly prepare and train for specific races, but what it actually did in Gary's case was create gaps in the season which he filled with as many races as he could get to. Racing for up to eight weeks in a row wasn't uncommon, and there were plenty of mid-week evening races in the summer. For Gary the sport wasn't as much about competition as about his lifestyle, and although he was aware that people were telling him he should race less, get a coach and run to a prescribed schedule, he stuck to his guns and just did what he wanted to do; which was run and race on the fells, whenever and wherever, and preferably with the rest of the Pudsey & Bramley team. He well understood that this gung-ho, raring-to-go attitude to racing wasn't necessarily beneficial to his running, and he knew that over-doing the less critical races risked failure in the more important races, just as he knew that his punk rock psyche would declare, loudly, that (in the words of Sex Pistols manager Malcolm McLaren):

"What matters is this: Being fearless of failure arms you to break the rules. I've always embraced failure as a noble pursuit. It allows you to be anti whatever anyone wants you to be, and to break all the rules."

The morning of the Three Peaks race was misty and dank, heavy and sodden underfoot. As the gun went to signal the start of the race, Gary was chewing over what was a common axiom that floated around the event every year: that the race didn't really start until Ribblehead, almost halfway into the 23-mile route. Completely ignoring this, Shaun went off like a shot, gapping the field as soon as they left the road out of Horton-in-Ribblesdale and haring up the lane towards Pen-y-Ghent, the first summit. Gary now had to make a snap decision; to chase after Shaun or to let him go and assume he would tire and blow up. Watching Shaun pulling away was too much temptation, and Gary decided to chase him down. He knew from the previous year's race – at which the pair had run neck-and-neck for most of the 23 miles before Shaun pulled away to win on the final climb up Ingleborough – that he could match Shaun over the route, and being Yorkshire-born he felt duty-bound to try to win such an iconic race, keeping his dad in bar-room bragging tales for the rest of his life. By the time they were halfway up the first big climb the two were well clear of the rest of the 800 runners ascending into the cloud.

The ground in the next section of the route around the aptly-named Dismal Hill was largely a huge brown swamp, every footstep sinking through the bent and broken reeds into the oozing gloopy quagmire beneath. From here, though, where the route followed farm tracks, the two settled into a rhythm and began chatting.

"Can you see anyone behind?"

"Nope. Nothing. Can't see anything in front, either."

"Like a training run this, isn't it?"

"It would be if you hadn't gone off so fast at the beginning."

"Someone told me there was £100 bonus for getting to the top of Pen-y-Ghent first."

"Anyway, since I let you win last year, how about giving me a couple of hundred yards start up Whernside?"

"You'll need it, my wife's waiting for me there with a hot coffee."

And on, and on, and on they went, matching each other step for step, barb for barb, along the stony tracks towards Ribblehead Viaduct and up the long, steep ascent of Whernside. The talking didn't stop, just ebbed and flowed, came and went, all the way across to the final climb at Ingleborough where the pair turned together at the summit cairn, still shrouded in cloud, supporters appearing out of the gloom to shout encouragement. On and on, chatter and gossip, twaddle and trivia, on and on and on and on until, as they hit the long rocky descent back towards Horton, Shaun stopped talking. Gary looked at him. Other than the pad of their feet and their heavy breaths, nothing. Gary understood what was happening; Shaun was tiring, and it was time to make a decisive move. As they clambered over a stile, a team-mate of Gary's – Jamie Smith, the self-styled loudest man in Yorkshire, with a voice like a foghorn and devoid of subtlety – yelled, *"You've got him, Gaaaaaaz! Go on, haaaaaaave him!"* And that's what Gary did, pulling away from Shaun and putting over a minute between them, becoming only the third Yorkshireman to win the race. Asked how he felt at the end of the race, Gary simply muttered, "I thought I ran better last year."

He had a point; all in all, it felt like he'd had a better season's racing the previous year. But sport is notorious for not being what you expect it to be, and the end of the decade seemed to come with a spirit of change. So far this year he hadn't won a Championship race and the races he had won he felt weren't his best performances. But perhaps, perhaps... one of the joys of sport is that sometimes the less-fancied and underrated can seize the anomaly, the irregularity, that changes the game. 'Fortune favours the brave', as some Ancient Greek philosopher said. Or as Dirty Harry put it, "Do you feel lucky, punk?"

CHAPTER 19

"You see
You feel
You know –
React!
You're waiting
We're waiting...
For change
Change!
Change!
Change!
Change!"
— Killing Joke, 'Change'

Killing Joke were a band who emerged from the fall-out of the first wave of punk in 1978 and created a unique and unforgettable noise. Drummer and co-founder Paul Ferguson described it as "the sound of the earth vomiting." Synthesisers and harsh metallic guitars crashed and rang alongside tortured vocals and heavy, tribal drumming. They took inspiration from the occult, and when they played live their leader Jaz Coleman would daub his face with warpaint. They were quite simply not like any other band, and even on Gary's 15-watt lo-fi stereo speakers they sounded grand, immense and scary. They were punk without the Mohican haircuts and safety pins, punk as a challenge to normality, punk as a rejection of tradition, and their song 'Change' was a call to arms, an anthemic, thunderous roar built around that one-word repeated chorus.

It was now almost a decade since some long-forgotten kid had lent

Gary the first Dead Kennedys album, and around a decade since an official had threatened Gary with being suspended from competing as an amateur for winning prize money at a junior fell race. These two light-bulb moments had illuminated the rest of his 1980s, setting a template for a life spent between ear-shatteringly loud gigs and halfway up a mountain at the front of a pack of several hundred runners. If he were to think about it, and thinking wasn't easy with Killing Joke's first album turned up full on the record player, he'd be able to acknowledge what an incredible time he'd had. Looking back, it would be clear that the two apparently opposing parts of his life weren't opposites at all but were complementary, two interlocking jigsaw pieces. Both rejected everyday humdrum routine. Both had given Gary a community, an identity and stability. But perhaps most importantly, both celebrated cherished adventure and wildness. Change!

The sport of fell and mountain running, with its proud traditions rooted in the history, culture and geography of Britain, was by 1990 being forced to confront how many of those traditions needed to be updated, changed or simply swept away. Tradition is a lovely thing until you realise that it can also be short-sighted and divisive, so along with a growing understanding of the environmental impact of the sport and how best to manage it, there were two issues in particular which had to be addressed, the most important being the proper integration of women into the sport.

Vocalist with righteous anarcho-punks Crass, Eve Libertine would take the mic and scream, a banshee with a cause howling at the top of her lungs, "You don't want a person, you just want a woman!" And the leather-jacketed boys in the crowd, the jostling, pogoing, joshing, spitting boys, they'd wonder what to make of it. Young and inexperienced, their version of women had come from urban and suburban family homes, they all-too-often didn't understand the anger and despair of this 1980s version of feminism and its demand for equality.

In 1979, French-born runner Véronique Marot decided she'd

like to run the classic Lakeland Ennerdale Fell Race. At the start line, the organisers informed her that she wasn't allowed to run on account of being a woman. She ignored them and ran anyway, without permission, much to the chagrin of the organisers and other runners. This wasn't the start of the struggle for women to be able to compete alongside men in fell races, but it marked a point when women had clearly had enough of competing 'quietly' in races and having their name and finishing time unlisted in the results.

Just after Véronique's run, in the early 1980s, three women – Joan Glass, Anne-Marie Grindley and Ann Bland – ran unofficially in the Ben Nevis race. A 'Ladies' Championship' was set up and women's fell racing became, as it developed through the 1980s, formalised and recognised, if not always greeted with open arms; the cat was out of the bag and couldn't be persuaded to go back in without a hell of a fight. Change!

Then there was the pulling down of the creaking barriers between the amateur and professional codes, a struggle which may have been soundtracked to Sham 69's shout-along chorus of, 'If the kids are united, they will never be divided…'. Knocking on teenagers' doors to warn them about their amateur status wasn't confined to Gary's particular neck of the shamateur woods. The suspensions and disqualifications had been going on for many years and as time went on it became increasingly obvious that the distinction between amateur and professional was nothing but a smokescreen to honour a hallowed tradition – a tradition that was set up to favour the middle- and higher-class athletes who could afford the time and expense of competing at a high level.

Even by the middle of the 1980s it seemed as if some sports – fell running among them – were stuck in a page from an 'Alf Tupper (Tough of the Track)' cartoon strip as seen in *The Victor* comic for several decades until the early 1990s: working-class lad, sleeves rolled up and smiling, labouring as a mechanic and seeming to survive on fish & chips. He's invited to race against the upper-class lads from the local public school, with their neat white kits and expensive spiked running shoes, and even though they habitually cheat, he beats them. Noble as this ideal was, it bore no relation to the reality of the so-called 'amateur' athletes earning hundreds of thousands of pounds on the international circuit, money which was put down as 'expenses' and paid into trust funds. The farce of Gary being warned for collecting £5 or £10 for winning junior fell races was clear.

The British Open Fell Racing Association (BOFRA) mainly ran its 'Open' professional races at a string of annual village fairs, traditional jamborees where a fell race competed with dog-handling, prize sheep and tug-of-war competitions alongside Women's Institute home-made cake sales. Where the atmosphere at these events was pleasantly welcoming, the races were aggressively competitive. Some of the races, though often very short, were among the toughest in both codes of the sport. Kilnsey Crag race is a short, sharp and dangerous race that leaves the showfield and crosses a river before climbing steadily to the local summit ridge overlooking the start and finish field. After a short run to the summit proper, the descent from the top is by way of a near-vertical drop through a crag face, where holding on to a wire fence adjoining a wall seemed to be the only way to avoid tumbling into a mess of rocks and scree. Each year runners complete the course sporting gashed and bloody knees, hands and elbows. It's a hell of a race, and every fell runner – amateur or professional – wants to race there.

The problem towards the end of the 1990s was that the runners – on both sides of the amateur/professional divide – were relatively happy to allow their counterparts to compete in 'their' races, while the organisers of both governing bodies were wary of doing so. The FRA was happy to make overtures to BOFRA (British Open Fell Running Association) but had one eye on what the Amateur Athletic Association would say to such a move. Meanwhile, many on the BOFRA committee were none-too-keen on admitting a huge slew of amateur runners into their world, into a social scene that was perfectly balanced by its own history and culture.

In the end, it didn't matter – those resisting change were overtaken by the tide of amateur runners who, sensing that the blazer 'n' tie AAA officials' days were numbered, began to turn up en masse to Open fell races and join in, kids in a sweet shop, excited to be running for the first time these classic, traditional races. The Berlin Wall between the two codes fell; or rather, was pulled down, for good. Change!

And in the real world… this was the year that Margaret Thatcher, tears in her eyes, finally left Downing Street for the last time. Seeing her popularity plummeting, and despite her assertion that she would "fight on and fight to win," her own party lanced the boil and installed John Major as their new leader. The backdrop to her fall was nationwide opposition to the Poll Tax, culminating in a huge riot as 200,000 people marched in central London and battled with police, to a soundtrack of the Roland TR-808 drum machine, an electronic box of repeated booms, snaps and sizzles. Change!

Gary was in his own world, for a while seemingly oblivious to this rhythmic beat of change, turning up the volume on his old records, running his races to punk's verse-chorus-verse-chorus patterns. But somehow, slowly, bit by bit by bit by bit, the drum machines and the synthesisers and the sampled wails and the looped noises wormed their way in, through the cracks opened up by punk's stasis, by punk's inability to move and change and develop. And Gary got hooked because he recognised and understood the repeating boom boom boom that came with the reports of illegal raves in open countryside, and he recognised music that came from urban and suburban bedrooms and basements and not from 48-track residential studios and cocaine boardrooms.

And here, again, was a music that could soundtrack his running, a simple 1, 2, 1, 2, binary digital beat, at 120 bpm heart-rate speed, a music that annoyed parents and drove the tabloids into a moral panic. If this year, 1990, could be typified as a time of change, then this was the intro music to that shift, that switch. The punk rock that had underpinned a decade of hill and mountain running still sounded as loud and as fast as ever, but now there was something else to run to.

Gary switched off the kettle and poured boiling water into a cup. He'd been working with his dad all day, refitting a cellar in Bramhope, putting in running water and drainage and mixing cement and lugging Yorkshire stone paving slabs up the street. He was knackered, but he knew if he relaxed and sat down for a minute he'd fall asleep and wake up to find the world had gone dark and it was 3am and he was wide awake. Instead he stirred milk into his tea, took off his boots and pulled a 12" vinyl record out of a carrier bag he'd brought with him. His room on Victoria Road, rented not squatted, had a bathroom with a working sink, a telephone that rang, locks on the doors, unbroken mirrors, a television with four channels and a fridge with a constant hum. In short, it was the kind of place that didn't get raided by the drug squad.

He looked at the record sleeve – blank, black, with a die-cut centre to reveal the record's label: Tommy Boy, green lines on a white background, simple Helvetica information: 808 STATE – B Side – IN YER FACE. He flipped open the lid of the record player and pushed the speed switch to 45RPM, placed the record on the turntable and lifted and lowered the needle into the shiny black plastic. Full volume. Synthesised, repeating patterns and an American voice intoning, *"There are new forces in the world… a new conflict between the generations…"* and a heavy piano riff banged into the mix before the bass drum kicked in, loud and thudding, electronic hi-hats rat-tat-tat-tatting across the beat. It didn't sound like punk or look like punk but… it smelled of punk. It smelled of the stuff that the *Daily Mail* screamed about, the counter-cultural stuff that gets up the nose of Middle England. And as far as Gary could tell, when you turned it up, all the way up, it rattled the same brain cells that punk could rattle. Boom boom boom boom boom.

Somewhere above the music, a voice was shouting.

"Gaaaary!"

"Gaaaary!"

Gary turned the music down. A bit. A little bit. The voice stayed outside the room, shouting through the closed door.

"Gaaaaary!"

"Yeah?"

"Oh it is you then. What's that shit?!"

"It's 808 State!"

"What?"

"808 State!"

"What's 808 State? Sounds like bloody rave music!"

Gary turned it down a notch at a time between each exchange. They were now talking at normal speaking volume, the music a low, fizzing soundtrack.

"Yeah. Well. It's not rave. It's techno."

"It's bloody crap is what it is. Are you going soft or what?"

"No. What's wrong with it?"

"Everything's wrong with it. But mainly what's wrong with it is that it isn't punk."

"Erm – Right. Thanks for your input."

The voice retreated across the hallway and started to climb the stairs. Gary turned the music back up. Turned it up to its limit. Then, opening the door, he let the music blare through the house. The voice paused and stopped on the top step.

"One word, mate –" the voice yelled, "– why?"

Gary yelled back, loud and with a smile in his voice.

"I fancied a change."

CHAPTER 20

1990 British Championship race 6
Ben Nevis Race, 1st September 1990
10 miles, 4400ft climb

"Chaos was the law of nature; Order was the dream of man."
— Henry Adams

Strange but somehow apt that it should all come down to this, to the final race of the Championship season and a cock-up in the entry system. Colin Donnelly, back from his trip to Switzerland to race at Davos, was told by the Fell Runners Association that, no, the Ben Nevis Race Committee would not change their entry policy and would not allow him to run the race. He was fuming. He'd never liked the race anyway, it seemed out of step with the ethos of hill running with its two-page list of rules and its secretive committee and its ridiculously high entry fee and its grand old prize-giving in its grand old hall. Missing both Snowdon and the Ben meant that he hadn't completed a medium race and so wouldn't be able to defend his Championship, which in turn meant that the chance was now there for this scruffy young pretender from Yorkshire to smash and grab the biggest prize in the sport.

How Gary saw it was that Colin had made the decision to race abroad instead of competing at Snowdon, on the assumption that the Ben Nevis Committee would buckle under pressure from the FRA to admit a late entry from an elite runner (and former winner of the race). And Gary thought, well, c'est la vie, shit happens, Murphy's

Law; to paraphrase the poet Robert Burns, the best-laid plans of mice and men often go awry. Gary had an inbuilt stoicism that meant he could glide over life's rougher patches with a faint grin and a shrug of the shoulders. The original Greek Stoics believed that the path to happiness was found in accepting the moment as it presented itself, by not allowing yourself to be controlled by either the desire for pleasure or the fear of pain. In other words, by achieving some sort of Zen-like equilibrium with the world; not a million miles from Gary's 'I don't care' punk nihilism. It is what it is.

After the International Snowdon race, Gary's dad Hughie was in the bar adjacent to the presentation ceremony, waiting in the melee to order a round of drinks and casting around for conversation – his lad had finished in the top ten, first non-international runner, and Hughie wanted to tell the world.

"Here, fella."

He caught the ear of a smart tracksuited man in his forties who was waiting beside him.

"Yes?"

"How you doing pal?"

"Pal? Yes, fine. And yourself?" The accent was foreign but crisp and eloquent.

"Oh aye. Great. My lad just came ninth in the race, I'm getting him and his mates a few drinks, like. To celebrate."

"Ninth? Oh, that is very good. He is running for England?"

"Nah. Didn't get picked. Running in his club colours. Pudsey and Bramley."

"Pudsley and Bramble?"

"No – Pudsey and – oh, never mind. And what are you here for, not from round here are you?"

"From Austria. I manage the Austrian team, we had a disappointing race overall but, you know, such lovely atmosphere and very welcoming people."

"Oh aye. Austria eh? Very nice. Proper mountains!"

"Oh yes. I live in part of Austria with very big mountains, many good races."

"You race?"

"No, I organise. I have races in my home town, there are many races in the area."

"Nice."

"You say your boy, he finished ninth?"

"That's right."

"Maybe we can invite him to compete on our mountains."

"Oh he'd love that. You say you organise races?"

"Yes. We could offer flights and accommodation for three, four days and entries to the races. What is his name?"

"Devine. Gary Devine. Lad with the bleached hair over there –" he pointed at Gary in among P&B's huddled group, away from the bar and dangerously close to a grand piano. "I tell you what," continued Hughie, "instead of all that stuff about flights, we could use the dosh to bring over a team, in the back of my van. Find us a floor to sleep on and chuck us some diesel money and I'll bring a little squad over."

Three weeks later the white van set off from Leeds full-to-bursting with runners, kit, sleeping bags, camping stoves, two crates of beer and Gary's brother Bradley. Along for the ride were Brian, Ady and Alan from Pudsey & Bramley and Andrew 'Scoffer' Schofield from Rochdale, always willing to throw his kitbag in the back of a van and see where he ended up. The trip to race at the 10-mile uphill-only road race in Kitzbühel somehow turned into a ten-day trip around Austria and Switzerland, with race organisers putting up these unexpected guests as they travelled round the continent following an incoherent zig-zag pattern of racing, drinking, racing, drinking, racing, drinking and racing. The only proviso was to arrive back in Britain in time for the Ben Nevis race at the start of September. Gary knew he could improve on his ninth position at Snowdon (his other medium counter) so was looking forward to the race. After his victory there in 1988 he'd given it a miss last year; Keith Anderson had won by a comfortable margin of over four minutes from Bingley's all-rounder Ian Ferguson.

At the end of the exhausting whistle-stop tour of the continent's various races and bars, Hughie's van finally criss-crossed its way back to Leeds, dropping off the exhausted and hung-over flotsam and jetsam of the trip at their houses before heading up Woodhouse Lane and alongside Hyde Park, a huge island of municipal green in the middle of an ocean of terraced red-brick.

"You can drop me here, Dad."

"No you're right, I can take you to your door."

"I'm not going straight home."

"Where are you off to? Thought you'd want to sleep for a week after all that."

"It's the Punk's Picnic. It'll just be getting going now. You can drop my stuff off at our house."

"Punk's Picnic? Shouldn't you be getting some shut-eye?"

Just then, speeding around the corner at the junction with Clarendon Road, a police car turned on its siren and its flashing blue light began to spin as it raced off up towards the north end of the park.

"See, I told you it was just getting going. See you next week for the Ben."

*

On the Tuesday, shortly after Gary had got home from some work building a fireplace in Pudsey, club-mate Alan Greenwood phoned up to pass on the news that neither Colin Donnelly nor Shaun Livesey were able to get an entry to the Ben Nevis race. The FRA had held a special meeting to try to resolve the situation, but their overtures to the intransigent Ben Nevis Committee had fallen on the deafest of ears. It was now up to Gary; he calculated that he would have to finish in the top three to win the overall British Championship.

So it all came down to this final race, and to add to the importance of it all, Pudsey & Bramley were in the closest of battles with Ambleside AC to see who would win the British Team Championship. They all travelled up to the Ben the night before and bunked in the Fort William Youth Hostel, sharing the evening streets with runners from right across Britain, all lured to the race by its history, its myths and its legendary toughness. Despite its reputation, fell runners knew deep down that it wasn't the toughest race in the calendar – that claim was better made for races at Wasdale, Ennerdale, the Isle of Jura, Arrochar Alps, Borrowdale, the Peris Horseshoe – but its notoriety outside the sport meant it was one to collect, a story to tell. Looking up at the mountain, neck craned to see the top, from the sea-level perspective of the Claggan Park football ground where the race begins and ends, was to appreciate the Ben's monumental grandness. For many of the 600 runners gathered for the race, being able to tell people outside the sport that you ran up and down that mountain (some in under two hours) would be an after-dinner story worth growing old with.

The first recorded run up and down the Ben was in 1895, when William Swan was timed racing to the summit and back in 2 hours 41 minutes. Swan, a local hairdresser, tobacconist, dog breeder and gad-about-town, fortified his run with a mountain-top cup of Bovril. When the race was formalised a few years later, ten runners competed and the winner was clocked at exactly the same time as Swan's original run. It's not possible to know how many of the races run between then and the present came with an actual view of the summit of Nevis, but a rough guess would be in the single figures. Ben Nevis is notoriously shy, shrouding itself in cloud for most of the year – a Gaelic translation of the origins of its name *(Beinn Nibheis)* is roughly 'mountain with its head in the clouds'.

The English Romantic poet Keats, aged just 22, climbed to its summit in 1818, a climb that was the culmination of a 600-mile walking tour. Having reached the bottom of the mountain after his ascent, he was advised by an Inverness physician to take a packet ship back to London to recover from a violent cold, an illness which dogged the remaining three years of his short life. But he'd come this far, and wasn't going to give this last climb a miss. At the summit, Keats wrote a short poem describing the mountain top, "blind in mist," as a place equally balanced between heaven and hell, the clouds swirling round about obscuring both. "All my eye doth meet is mist and crag, not only on this height, but in the world of thought and mental might!"

The morning of the race dawned in the manner of many a Fort William morning, with a light drizzle. By now Gary had worked out who would be running and who he needed to beat, having bumped into most of them somewhere along Fort William's main street the previous night. He'd avoided any late-night drinking (well, mostly) and slept easily in a dormitory of snoring, belching and farting runners before casually walking up to Craggan Park and the start of the race. Ambleside's Keith Anderson was there and looked sharp and fit, alongside Scottish internationals Mark Rigby and David Rodgers – Gary had beaten Rodgers at both Eildon and Snowdon, but Rodgers' fourth place at last year's Ben proved he enjoyed this kind of race. Rigby excelled at the longer, tougher courses, having won that year's Wasdale race, and the rocky, bouldered and dangerous descent from Ben Nevis summit played to Keith Anderson's strengths.

Usually Gary wouldn't be over-concerned about the importance of a race – he'd do his best, he'd near-kill himself to go faster, but he'd enjoy it, he'd get to the finish with a smile on his face. Today, unusually, was different. People were asking him if he thought he could "do it." And for the first time in as long as he could remember, he began to feel nervous – not the sort of pre-race nerves that disappear as soon as you're off and away, but a strange, unpleasant nervous energy that, even as they stood on the start line ready for the off, told him that this wasn't fun.

Off they went, along the tarmac road to Achintee and onto the hill proper, with Mark Rigby out in front, determined to strike out on the climb in the knowledge that both Gary and Keith were better technical descenders. Conditions were now dry and cool, the sections of uneven stone slabs twisting around the valley and up, up, up to the Red Burn, the halfway point. From just beyond the Burn the race cuts up sharply to the zig-zagging path laid in loose, bleached rock and on up to the summit plateau, shrouded in light mist, where Gary and Keith ran together, Gary just behind and looking back to see that they had a reasonable lead over the chasing pack. Rigby reached the summit cairn in the lead, then turned and retraced his steps, fully two minutes up on Keith and Gary, determined to build up enough of a lead to prevent being caught.

And there, over beyond the mountaintop cairn and sitting beside the ruins of the old Observatory, sat John Keats, watching the runners approaching, notebook in one hand and pencil in the other. As they came closer they could see that he looked pale, unsmiling, intermittently scribbling ideas in his book and looking beyond the pair towards the thin curtain of cloud behind them. Gary had experiences of flashbacks and hallucinations; years ago he'd taken mushrooms and LSD and knew how the human brain can construct its own version of what's real, can turn the world inside-out and upside-down, right-side-up and backwards-round. But there he was, really – John Keats, young, intense, black frock coat and knotted collared shirt, watching a foot-race, occasionally coughing. Etching out the lines to a poem, writing and re-writing and crossing out and starting again, 'The sermon's horrid sound...', written to a rhythm of pounding drums and rumbling bass, a sound Gary recognised – the tribal yell of 'No Gods, No Masters' by Amebix. The wind picked up and blew across the flat and open summit, momentarily blowing the clouds off into thin air, taking poet, poem and punk music into the ether.

Gary dug in, knowing that he had to stick with Keith as long as he could, realising that once they hit the rocky descent through the zig-zags he probably wouldn't be able to match Keith's daredevil approach to downhill running. Coming out of the clouds, Keith did precisely that – pulled away in a scrambled flurry of rock and studded shoes, leaping across the shifting rocks and boulders and bracing against the steep angle of descent. By the foot of the zig-zagging path Gary was on his own, tumbling down the sodden and treacherous grassy bank toward the Red Burn. Third place. He looked back: Davey Rodgers was in sight, reaching the top of the grass section and gradually closing. Again, Gary thought to himself: this isn't fun. He felt anxious, he cared too much, the uneasiness was turning into doubt.

Down the long tourist path, with its angled steps and narrow bridges, hopping from foot to foot to clear the twists and turns in the trail, Gary reached the final half a mile of tarmac that led back to the finishing field. Another glance backwards and Davey was getting closer. Gary's legs, shattered from the brutal descent, weren't responding, and there was a slowly rising sickness in his stomach. It wasn't panic, or fear – it was that nagging feeling of caring too much, of knowing what this third place would mean. His thoughts of running along the road and comfortably securing the Championship were evaporating and all he could think was *shit!* And the word repeated itself *shit!* and again *shit!* and again *shit!* until he reached the football field, ran through the gates and looked back one more time – one more time *shit!* and there was Davey, ten seconds behind, catching as Gary forced a desperate, heavy-legged sprint – nine seconds, eight seconds, 100 metres of the circuit left to race, seven seconds, six seconds – and Gary collapsed as he crossed the line, hearing Davey Rodgers right behind him. He'd done it.

EPILOGUE

"When I buy a new book, I always read the last page first, that way in case I die before I finish, I know how it ends."
– Nora Ephron, When Harry Met Sally

Almost three decades later and it's a harsh, windswept, freezing day up on the mountains north of Sedbergh in North Yorkshire. A hundred runners – including me – line up and set off running towards the cloud-covered summit of Boar Fell, in a race that's kept deliberately low-key. It isn't in the official race calendar and it isn't to be found online; it's word-of-mouth only. It's a credit to the organisers that anyone is here at all. In fact it's organised by Gary and Debbie Devine, who arrange this race every year on an annual visit to England from their home in the French Alps. The date isn't given out until two weeks before it happens; Gary's friends and family gather to set up registration and take down results.

Up at the top of Boar Fell there's a thick cloud that threatens to send disorientated runners off the sheer edge of the ridge. It's truly wild up here, with very low visibility and a swirling wind that pushes and pulls you this way and that. Everyone desperately keeps the runner in front in their sights to avoid getting utterly lost in the dense mist and torrential rain. Suddenly, as the mountain top crests to its summit, I just about make out a figure, wrapped in a huge waterproof and standing beside a slowly-emerging trig point. At his feet there's a dog, or at least the hazy shape of a dog. As I approach the figure it becomes clear that it's Gary, chuckling drily through the rain, passing casual insults to each runner as they reach the summit and begin to descend. He sees it's me and shouts,

"What took you?"

Here he is, still out on the fells, cheeky, belligerent, happy, searching for different adventures, maybe not wearing those old rotting T-shirts but definitely still wearing that *No Gods, No Masters* tattoo on his arm. As I turn to face the long descent off the summit, I remember what I'd come up here for, and stop.

"I've got something for you, Gary."

"What?"

He's wondering now, why on earth would I stop, up here in the teeth of a gale in the middle of a race, to start a conversation? I swivel my bumbag around so I can get at the zip, my freezing fingers tugging it open. A runner behind me catches up and passes, wordless, breathing heavily, wondering what's going on. I grab at something.

"Here, I brought you this."

I pull out an A4 sheaf of papers, loosely bound together with a plastic clip and rolled to fit in the bag. I hold it out but keep a tight grip, scared of the intense wind that's battering us on the exposed top of the mountain.

"What is it?"

"It's a manuscript. Here, take it."

Even the dog is taking an interest now. Maybe she thinks I have something else more exciting than a manuscript. A biscuit, a ball, a pat on the head.

"It's a manuscript for a book. It's about you. About you winning the British Championship back in 1990. And about fell running and punk rock, about those two extremes. The conflict between the discipline and focus of running and the unruliness and adventure of punk. And inversely, about the chaotic joy of fell running and the rhythmic order and structure of punk rock. Why the two things are so different – but also why they're so alike."

Gary looks at me below his dripping cagoule hood, looks at me like I'm mad. He catches hold of the rolled papers, his gloved fingers fumbling to keep a good hold.

A mighty blast of wind draws itself up, huge and loud and strong, before hammering us both, sucker-punching us. The dog yelps, bewildered, and as Gary turns to look towards her, his hold on the papers loosens, slips, fumbles. The pages unclip and tear for release, one by one, a rapid-fire explosion of printed sheets that fly up and out with the wind, soaring and scattering and sailing away over the summit's edge and off on their separate twisting journeys towards the Pennines, the coast and the North Sea, up into the storming sky and right across the world, upwards and eastwards, leaving behind two blokes on a mountaintop, laughing.

ACKNOWLEDGEMENTS

It goes without saying that some of the events and dates detailed in this book are historically inaccurate. It was never meant to be a detailed and perfectly memorised roll-call of race results and concert reviews. Having said that, all this stuff did actually happen and in roughly this sequence.

Thanks go first and foremost to Gary (of course) and to all the people I interviewed, for helping out with stories, details, dates and names. Those people were:

For the punk side of things – Dev, Sarah Devlin, Ben Swarbrick, Danbert Nobacon, and especially Jan Shaw for all sorts of mad stories and reminiscences.

For the running stuff – Richard Pallister, Ady Illingworth, Jack Maitland, Terry Lonergan, Norman Berry and Pete Bland. Ever-helpful and enthusiastic, Pete sadly died during the writing of this book.

Thanks to those who read early versions of the book and offered comments and edits – Graham Pilling, Richard Jobson, Josh Sutton, Billy Bland, Richard Askwith, Damian Hall, Casey Orr and Christian Brett.

Thanks to Dan Bye for the continuing philosophical running conversations, and to Rose George and Jay Griffiths for inspiration.

Thanks to Gary's brother Bradley for various asides and clarifications, and his mum for the photographs. Thanks to Debbie Devine for operating the technology that Gary didn't know how to use!

Thanks to Jan Shaw for most of the punk photographs, and thanks to Denise Parks for allowing us to use the photograph of Gary at the World Cup event by the late legendary fell running photographer Peter Hartley.

Thanks to Steve Chilton and Graham Breeze for their various writings on the history of fell running, its characters and its organisation.

Thanks to both *Up & Down* magazine and *The Fell Runner* magazine for invaluable contemporary race reports and results, and especially to Dave and Eileen Woodhead for being ever-present and encouraging.

Thanks to Eileen Jones for reference to the piece she wrote for the *Yorkshire Post* in 1989.

Thanks to David Luxton, agent, who found a home for this strange idea for a book, and to David Burrill and Peter Crangle at Great Northern Books. Thanks to Ross Jamieson for proofing.

Thanks to my dad Jim for convincing me to go and watch the Simon's Seat fell race in 1986 (and thus condemning me to a lifetime of mud, exhaustion and joy).

And thanks to Casey, Maisy and Johnny for running (always running!) through everything with me.

Gary would like to thank:

Mum and Dad, all Pudsey & Bramley runners and fell runners from the 1980s, Terry Lonergan, Jan, Leeds Punks, all the punk bands around at the time, Debbie and Leah for putting up with all the reminiscing, and finally Boff.